THE DÜSSELDORF VAMPIRE

THE SADIST
By Dr. Karl Berg

PUBLISHING HISTORY
"DER SADIST," JULIUS SPRINGER VERLAG
BUCHHANDLUNG, 1932.
"THE SADIST," ACORN PRESS, 1938. Translated by Olga
Illner and George Godwin.
"THE DÜSSELDORF VAMPIRE," KORSGAARD
PUBLISHING, 2020. REISSUE.

This edition of "THE SADIST" contains the original 1938
translation by Olga Illner and George Godwin. Two pictures
from the 1938 hardcover edition were not retrievable. The text
has been edited accordingly. Minor typographical and
editorial errors have also been corrected. Book formatting by
Lady Jane Emefa Addy. Design and editing by Søren Roest
Korsgaard.

TABLE OF CONTENTS

<u>FOREWORD</u>

In the annals of crime, Peter Kürten's thirst for death and destruction remains unparalleled, despite that nearly one hundred years have passed since he walked to the guillotine in the early morning hours of July 2, 1931, in the Klingelpütz Prison. Shortly before the executioner released the blade that severed Kürten's head from his body, Kürten had asked Dr. Karl Berg, a professor of forensic medicine at the Düsseldorf Medical Academy, the question: "Tell me, after my head is chopped off, will I still be able to hear, at least for a moment, the sound of my own blood gushing from the stump of my neck? That would be the pleasure to end all pleasures." Kürten's unmatched ability to inflict horror and destruction had no limits. He habitually indulged in bestiality, rape, necrophilia, murder, and delighted in drinking blood from humans and sometimes animals. This earned him the nickname: *The Düsseldorf Vampire.* Kürten's criminal and murderous inclinations overwhelmed him for the first time at an early age when he murdered two of his childhood friends. But 1925 became a turning point when he returned to Düsseldorf. On the night of his arrival, he observed, "The sunset was blood-red on my return." Kürten, an avid reader of newspaper articles on murder and gore, knew that the sky over London in 1888 during Jack the Ripper's reign of terror was blood-red. He later admitted, "I considered this to be an omen symbolic of my destiny." And that destiny was murder. His evil spirit led him to commit a series of arsons and rapes, and in 1929 it culminated into what has become known as the *Year of Terror.*

After his arrest, Dr. Berg earned the trust of Kürten, who confessed the full range of his crimes to him and went into details about his personal reflections and motivations, holding nothing back. Following the execution of Kürten, Dr. Berg collected his notes and analyses and began writing. In 1932, he published his invaluable forensic and psychiatric analyses of Kürten under the title, *Der Sadist.*

The book was written in German, and in 1938, translators, Olga Illner and George Godwin, made it available to the English market, under the title, *The Sadist*. Since then, the book went out of print and its copyright expired. *The Sadist* contains unique insights into the mind, methods, and madness of Peter Kürten. Recognizing that the book still has contemporary significance, the task of republishing it was undertaken in 2020.

While the psychology of Kürten is of interest to professionals in psychology, psychiatry, and law enforcement, his psychodynamics are also of interest to true crime readers who want to better understand the darkest of human behaviors. Illuminating the driving forces that propel people to commit atrocities is, however, not limited to studying convicts as is the norm. Understanding the full spectrum of evil requires an analysis of behaviors which are within the legal framework of one's country, behaviors which to some are acceptable, even normal, but to others are criminal and evil. Once we realize the "paradox of good and evil," as we may call it, the discussion becomes exceedingly complex and controversial. Nevertheless, it is clear that using legality as the standpoint of right and wrong is a fallacy as some of the most horrendous atrocities in world history were meted out in the name of the law. In 1795, Marquis de Sade, the father of sadism, described the relativistic nature of good and evil in his magnum opus, *La Philosophie dans le Boudoir*, in this dialogue:

> **Eugenie:** But it would however appear to me that there must be actions in themselves so dangerous and so evil that they have come to be considered from one end of the earth to the other as generally criminal.
> **Madame de Saint-Ange:** There are none, my love, none, not even theft, nor incest, neither murder nor parricide itself.
> **Eugenie:** What! such horrors are somewhere tolerated?
> **Dolmance:** They have been honored, crowned, beheld as exemplary deeds, whereas in other places,

humanness, candor, benevolence, chastity, in brief, all our virtues have been regarded as monstrosities!

Kürten, himself, evil and brutal to an extent outside the imagination of even the most creative writers of fiction, passed moral judgment on abortionists, whom he said had a much higher death toll than he. Kürten recognized the paradox of himself having committed murders without conscience and regret, yet felt bitter at other criminals as he saw them:

> As I now see the crimes committed by me, they are so ghastly that I do not want to attempt any sort of excuse for them. Still, I feel some bitterness when I think of the physician and the lady physician in Stuttgart who have been encouraged by a section of the community to murder and who have stained their hands with human blood to the extent of fifteen hundred murders.

The question is: Why is it that Kürten and others within and outside the law are able to carry through with their actions without the least bit of guilt, doubt, or apprehension? In court, the judge asked Kürten as to whether or not he had any conscience. Kürten calmly replied:

> I have none. Never have I felt any misgiving in my soul; never did I think to myself that what I did was bad, even though human society condemns it. As I have figured it out, when I am executed, my blood and the blood of my victims will be on the heads of my torturers, that is if there is such a thing as a Higher Justice. I have thought of the law of cause and effect, and on the law of the sufficient motive. There must be a Higher Being who gave in the first place the first vital spark to life. That Higher Being would also deem my actions good since I revenged injustice. The punishments I have suffered have destroyed all my

feelings as a human being. That was why I had no pity for my victims.

The answer to the question is that Kürten felt justified. Similarly, Kürten's executioner, who probably killed dozens of condemned men, perhaps even hundreds, he, too, most likely felt justified, even proud, and was convinced that he did the right thing. Since the days of Kürten, forensic science has evolved immensely. DNA analysis and many other highly advanced investigative methods are at the disposal of detectives and are routinely used to convict and acquit when cases go to court. Nevertheless, it is well established that innocent people are occasionally beheaded, hanged, lethally injected or shot in a long list of countries that still support capital punishment. This indicates with a high degree of certainty that Kürten's executioner, himself, was a coldblooded killer, having unleashed the blade of the guillotine upon men or women who were innocent of the crime for which they were sentenced to death. So what are really the moral and psychological differences between Kürten and his executioner, not to mention between Kürten and those who cheer for capital punishment?

Søren Roest Korsgaard (b. 1986) is a social critic, humanitarian, entrepreneur, and author. He serves as the editor-in-chief of www.crimeandpower.com. Søren is the founder of the editorially independent, pro-free speech publishing house, *Korsgaard Publishing* (KP). editor@crimeandpower.com

CHAPTER I
THE DÜSSELDORF ATROCITIES, 1929

In the whole history of crime there is to be found no record comparable in circumstances of frightfulness with the long series of crimes perpetrated in our own time by the Düsseldorf murderer, Peter Kürten.

The epidemic of sexual outrages and murders which took place in the town of Düsseldorf between the months of February and November in the year 1929, caused a wave of horror and indignation to sweep, not only through Düsseldorf, but through all Germany and, it may be said without exaggeration, throughout the whole world.

As one outrage succeeded another and always in circumstances of grim drama; as one type of crime was followed by yet another, public consternation reached the point of stupefaction.

Kürten, however, has been judged; he now belongs to criminal history.

Kürten's crimes were not merely the subject of exhaustive judicial examination; justice went deeper in his case and sought to probe the soul of this strange and enigmatic man. In so doing Justice has placed us in a position to understand the nature both of the crimes and of the perpetrator of them. Here, for the medico-jurist, is truly absorbing material for study, for Kürten is a clinical subject who yields, in exchange for a careful analysis, a real enlargement of our knowledge of the abnormal operating in the sphere of crime. I have arranged the extensive material in the following pages in the following way. I shall first deal with and describe, from the medico-legal standpoint, the events which took place in Düsseldorf in 1929. I shall then proceed to deal with the crimes as they were described to me by the criminal himself, and, last, I shall attempt an analytical estimate of the criminal and the nature of his crimes in the light of our knowledge of sadism.

I propose first to describe the state of affairs disclosed by my investigations, later I shall offer an interpretation of them in the light of knowledge later acquired of the perpetrator.

THE MURDER OF THE OHLIGER CHILD.

Case 46. On the 9th of February, 1929, about 9 o'clock in the morning, workmen going to work found in the vicinity of the building upon which they were employed in the Kettwiger-strasse, in the Flingern district, the body of an eight-year-old girl lying under a hedge. The ground at that point sloped slightly towards the hedge, and as the hedge faced a wide open space, it was only by chance that the body was discovered.

The body was completely clothed and clad in a cloak. The clothing, however, was partially burnt and the underclothing still smouldered. The body, which smelled strongly of petroleum, was not in any sort of disorder, for even the openings of the dress and the knickers were not disarranged. A closer examination of the clothing revealed bloodstains from multiple wounds in the breast, wounds made, quite obviously, through the clothing. On the inner part of the knickers near the external genitalia were two small bloodstains. Microscopic examination revealed the presence here, about of seminal fluid. In the vagina there was fluid blood which had flowed from a wound 1 cm. in length, at the entrance of the vaginal cavity.

The autopsy showed that the burning had affected practically only the clothing, injuring the skin surface no where but on the upper part of the thighs, the neck and chin, over which area the skin was blackened and discoloured, while the hair of the head was a black, charred mass, here and there completely burnt off. On the left breast there was a group of thirteen wounds, the face was bloated and livid. The stabs about the left breast were grouped over an area rather smaller than a hand. Five of the wounds had penetrated the heart, three had pierced the left and right pleurae; three had penetrated the liver. In the pleural cavities I found 750 cc. of blood. Death must have been swift through internal haemorrhage. The scene of the crime was without trace of blood. The criminal had attempted to burn the clothing of the body only. There were no traces to suggest that soot had been inhaled, and the burning was without vital reaction. In the tissues of the lumbar region there was some 4 cm. of blood infiltration. In the stomach was found a mass of chyme, partially digested white cabbage, and remains of meat.

The essential factors to be considered, from the medico-legal standpoint, for a diagnosis of the cause of death and for a theory as to the time of it, as well as for the motive of the murderer, were the characteristic stabs, the congestion of blood which was found in the head, the exact nature of the wounds and the condition of the contents of the stomach, and, last, the injury to the genitalia. So far as the congestion of blood in the head is concerned, one can only suggest that it indicated a forcible strangulation.

The judicial autopsy of the Ohliger child established the time of death, the contents of the stomach assisting to that end. Death must have occurred very quickly through the heart wounds. There were no visible marks strangulation must have initiated the attack though leaving no traces on the skin of the neck. No calls for help were heard in the rather populous neighbourhood where the crime was committed.

The mother deposed that the murdered child had eaten sauerkraut about 2 p.m. and had then set out to visit a friend. At 6 o'clock the friend had advised the child to hurry home before dark. There was a public footpath which she could take and which offered her a short cut.

Bearing in mind the fact that in six hours the stomach could normally complete the work of digestion, then the scarcely digested food found in the stomach indicates that death took place between 6 and 7 o'clock in the evening. The autopsy indicated that the child had been waylaid while on her homeward way.

The condition of the genitals revealed an injury of little consequence on the mucous membrane of the vagina. The hymen was torn about 1 cm. Only slight traces of seminal fluid were found on the child's under clothing. It was clear that an ejaculation could not have taken place into the vagina. From these considerations I arrived at the conclusion that the criminal's objective had not been coitus, but that he must have

inserted a finger smeared with semen under the unopened
knickers of the child and thus inserted it into the vagina. This
must have been done with force, for in addition to the scratch
at the entrance of the vagina, there was also a trace of bruising
of the pelvis.

The stabs in the skin of the breast were all together and
parallel. Some of these showed that the knife had been held
with the cutting edge of the blade upwards. I concluded from
the position of these wounds that the criminal had done the
stabbing in the breast as the child lay unconscious on the
ground, delivering the blows in swift succession. Otherwise
one would have expected that the stabbings inflicted on a
person still conscious would have been placed irregularly. In
addition one would expect to find defensive wounds on the
hands.

That my conclusions were correct is borne out by the attack
which took place on an elderly woman and of which I learned
only later. This attack took place five days before the murder
of Rosa Ohliger. I attributed it immediately to the same
criminal, an assumption which was to be confirmed by later
events.

FRAU KÜHN.

Case 45. At 9 p.m. on the 3rd of February, 1929, Frau Kühn
was waylaid at dusk on a lonely road in the Flingern district.
The man overtook her, bid her "Good evening," gripped her
by the lapels of her coat with the words: "No row! Don't
scream!" With the other hand he stabbed her. The woman fell
back and screamed for help. The criminal made off.

I found in the case of Frau Kühn twenty-four flesh wounds on
the head, the trunk, and the arms. The victim said that the
criminal had stabbed her in rapid succession.

In the case of the third victim (Case 47) there were the same
numerous stabs, characteristic of the same criminal. Only five
days after the murder of Rosa Ohliger there was found on the
Hellweg, on the out-skirts of the town, and once again in the
Flingern district, the body of a man, by name Scheer, of about
forty-five years of age. He had sustained twenty knife

wounds, of which sixteen were over a small area of the neck. Except for one stab, all were horizontal. Only one stab in the neck and three in the back were vertical. Three stabs had proved fatal: a stab in the temple had caused severe haemorrhage into the brain cavity, the stab in the neck had caused bleeding into the spinal cord, and the stab in the back had resulted in a pneumo-thorax. From the absence of defensive wounds, and from the distribution of the stabs, I drew the conclusion that the criminal had attacked his victim from behind and stabbed him.

Scheer had left a beer-house in the evening in a drunken state. He must have been attacked between 11 o'clock and midnight, but not until the next morning about 8 o'clock was the body found. Despite a temperature of 62° F. the body was still warm, *rigor mortis* just setting in. The combination of stabs, alcohol and low temperature explains the slow death. At the time when these three attacks took place, all within the short space of ten days, there was no clue whatever to the criminal. The only positive data were given by the findings of the medico-legal experts as follows; a comparison of the three cases revealing them as having the following characteristics in common:

(1) Sudden attack in isolated parts of Flingern.

(2) The choice of dusk; numerous stabs of the same character, among which always one stab in the temple, and all executed in rapid succession.

(3) The employment of same sort of stabbing instrument.

(4) Absence of a common motive – robbery, etc. All these factors, taken together, make inevitable the conclusion that the same criminal committed the three crimes and, furthermore, the abnormal character of the criminal.

It was fatal for the detection of this criminal that exactly six weeks later an imbecile named Stausberg appeared on the scene with two attacks on women which had some similarity to the crimes described above and thus confused the issue. I cite them here although they have nothing to do with Kürten himself. Again, there were similar circumstances: dusk, a lonely place on the outskirts of the town, a silent assault, an attempt to kill.

THE STAUSBERG CASES.

The sixteen-year-old Erna Penning was on her way home on the evening of the 2nd of April, 1929, when she suddenly heard steps behind her. Thinking it was her friend, she put up her coat collar in a spirit of fun in order to render herself unrecognizable, holding it close with both hands. That action saved her life, for at that moment a noose was thrown over her head.

I now quote her own words as to what followed: "I had my hands under the cord and with all my strength I tried to prevent the man from tightening the noose. I saw that he was very excited and that he was making great efforts to tighten the noose. I stumbled into the ditch towards the bank. The man held the noose together with one hand while with the other he throttled me. He threw me on to my back, fell to his knees beside me and kept on strangling me. I caught hold of his nose and pinched the nostrils together. In a last effort I succeeded in getting up. The man stepped back and took the rope off. He didn't speak a word. I ran away."

Twenty-four hours later came the second attack upon Frau Flake. Here is her account of it.

"On the 3rd of April, 1929, I was walking from the place where I used to work in the north part of the town by an ill-lit street. I heard steps behind me and saw a man coming. I walked more slowly in order to let him pass. The man must have jumped at me very quickly because suddenly something was flung over my head and I was jerked violently backwards. I was pulled from the road into the field. I could not shout, for the man had tried to push a handkerchief into my mouth. I clenched my teeth. He said, half aloud: 'Open your mouth.' He tightened the loop still more. Then he listened to see whether I still breathed and held his hand in front of my mouth. He then hauled me another ten meters. I heard steps approaching and tried to shout, but I couldn't. I struggled with my legs. It was then that I was released and the man turned and ran away across the fields. I loosened the loop and dragged myself towards some people who were standing in the road."

From this witness's statement it was clear that a dangerous attack had taken place. The attack had been witnessed by a man from a distance. He deposed as follows:

"When I approached I saw that a man was dragging a woman behind him across the fields. She was not on all-fours, but was being literally dragged along the ground." The medical report, made the following day, revealed the serious nature of this assault. Frau Flake was not able to swallow properly. On her neck she had a large, very red swelling 7 cm. long by $\frac{3}{4}$ cm. wide. On the left a painful reddish mark 5 cm. long and 3 cm wide. The skin of the whole face was covered with contusions in size from a pin point to a pea. The conjunctivae of both eyes were partly congested. In the mucous membrane of the mouth were numerous abrasions.

The criminal had been seen running away from the assaulted woman, and he was very soon identified. He was the twenty-year-old Stausberg, the imbecile son of a family lodging in a common lodging-house. It was difficult to interrogate Stausberg because, having an impediment in his speech, he spoke in broken sentences.

I reproduce his account of the two attacks mainly in his own words. First his comments on the Penning assault:

"The girl was a head taller than I am. She had put up the collar of her coat — a fur coat. Therefore, I wasn't able to tighten the rope. I had the rope with me. At one end I had made a noose, and at the other a loop for my hand. When I saw the girl I took the noose from my pocket and threw it over her head. She struggled and kicked and cried out for help. I, too, was on the ground."

Of the attack on Frau Flake, he said: "I saw her going along. I was furious. I had got the rope all ready and threw it from behind over her head. I took my handkerchief, said: 'Open your mouth.' I did not pull her along by the cord. It was under her armpits. I only attacked her because I had a grievance."

Stausberg must be regarded as proved guilty by his surprisingly accurate account of minute details of the two attacks, on the one side, and the objective data on the other. Naturally, nothing was more simple than to accuse Stausberg of the three February attacks. His comments upon them were, indeed, startling. He knew so many details that he could not have known from the newspapers, being an illiterate. So it came about that he was suspected of having committed these crimes, and this despite certain grave doubts.

The attack on Frau Kühn he described as follows: "I had gone to Gerresheim to look for work. Then I walked. A woman was walking in front of me. It was dark. I gripped her on the breast and stabbed the woman first in her head, then I went on stabbing. Blood came immediately after the first stab. She fell down. I stabbed into her heart. She shouted for help. I ran away. I couldn't help it."

The death of Rosa Ohliger he describes, but with discrepancies when compared with the facts of my medical report. "The child came towards me. I said: 'You come with me.' The child didn't say anything. She went with me up to the church. It was dark. I did not see any people. I took out my knife and stabbed. First in the head [indicating the right temple], then I held the child and stabbed her [with his left hand he grips the coat of the investigating police officer near the neck and with his right hand he executes rapid stabbing movements towards the left breast]. Then I kept stabbing. Then the child fell down and was dead immediately. I hadn't stabbed more than three times. When the child was lying on the ground I didn't stab any more. That is quite certain. That is not a lie. Then I listened a bit, whether the child still breathed. And then I left her lying ... I went to a shop and asked for a litre of petroleum. I paid twenty pfennig for it. I went back and poured the petroleum over the clothing. But not all of it. Some petroleum remained in the bottle. I set it afire with a match to the coat. The flame was high up to the knee. At home I washed the blood from my coat. My mother asked me where the blood came from. I said from my nose."

(When the next day the murder had been reported in the papers, Stausberg's mother had asked him whether he was the culprit. He answered "Yes, I certainly did it." His mother told him to "keep his mouth shut.")

"You see that I can also keep my mouth shut." Last, his description of the murder of Scheer. "It was late in the evening. I was out with a friend. I wanted to drink beer. When I wanted to pay the tavern-keeper said: 'It's all right.' Outside the inn he said to me: 'You scoundrel.' He swayed. He came towards me. I don't take anything from anybody. He wanted to punch my nose. I don't let anybody punch my nose. I took my knife from my pocket and stabbed him. He was done for. He fell over right away. I always hit on the head and then that does the job. He wanted to give me a shove. I caught hold of him from behind. I don't let any fellow talk to me. I don't stand anything from a girl either. He fell on his face. He felt in his pocket and found a knife which I took from him. I think I left it lying there. The others say I am a little devil. I don't stand for anything, and then I see red. I took the knife from him otherwise he would have killed me."

At a later hearing of the case: "I gave him a stab in the neck, then I kept on stabbing. A stab on the side of the head. Then he fell over. I listened once and then I cleared out. It is the same knife as with the woman and the child. Later I lost the knife."

When the real criminal had been detected there was a tendency to reproach the police officials for suspecting Stausberg. But as Stausberg had proved his propensity for homicidal impulsive acts through his two attacks, his accusation of himself was, with reason, regarded as credible. It is a valuable addition to our knowledge that an imbecile who is almost a complete idiot can invent so thorough and deceptive a false confession.

Stausberg's prosecution was stopped under paragraph 51 of the Criminal Code and he was removed to a lunatic asylum. In August, however, there were further attacks by a "ripper," despite the elimination of the supposed murderer. These crimes differed entirely from the crimes of the idiot and this

13

circumstance supported the theory that Stausberg was, indeed, guilty of those crimes to which he confessed, even where there was no corroboration. Thus these new atrocities were attributed to some unknown perpetrator or perpetrators.

THE KNIFE ATTACKS OF AUGUST, 1929.

On the 21st of August, 1929, in the western suburb of the town of Lierenfeld, three people were stabbed while walking home at night.

Case 55. In the vicinity of a church square a Frau Mantel was accosted by a stranger. He said: "May I accompany you, Fräulein?" Frau Mantel making no reply was rewarded by a stab in the back.

Case 54. Round about the same time a stranger approached Anna Goldhausen and, without speaking a word, gave her a stab which penetrated between the sixth and seventh ribs, penetrated both liver and stomach and incapacitated her for a long time.

Case 56. Again, about the same hour, and in the same quarter of the town, a man named Heinrich Kornblum was accosted and stabbed in the back. In this case the knife had, in one instance, cut the victim's braces, a circumstance which resulted in the perfect impression of a knife stab, and, hence, the shape and dimensions of the blade, 15 mm. On these data I came to the conclusion that the knife used in this case was not that used in the case of the Ohliger child or in that of the man Scheer. This seemed to be but one more ground for suspecting some culprit other than Stausberg.

The murder of Gross, which took place between the last-named two crimes, strengthened my belief in the theory that we had to seek more than one culprit.

On the night of the 30th of July, 1929, the thirty five-year-old prostitute Gross was found naked and strangled on the divan in a house of convenience. She showed no wounds except the characteristic marks of strangulation on the neck. This case differed but little from the fairly frequent murders of prostitutes common to all large towns; for it happens, often enough, that these women are killed in the course of their profession.

There was nothing about this case to incline me to the view that it was another committed by the same unknown as in the previous cases under investigation. Indeed, up to this very day the murder of Gross remains an unsolved crime. Incidentally, Kürten had nothing to do with it.

Again, the types of crime which took place at Flehe were of yet another category as will appear. These involved the five-year-old child Gertrude Hamacher and her fourteen-year-old adopted sister, Louisa Lenzen.

They had gone to the market place on Saturday evening and had failed to return home. During that night a search was made for them in every public place and thoroughfare between the market-place of Flehe and their lodgings which were not far off, but in vain.

The following Sunday morning at 6 o'clock their bodies were found on the market garden, only 200 metres from their lodgings. The younger child, Hamacher, was found lying among some runner beans; the elder, Lenzen, lay some seventeen metres away on a freshly turned vegetable bed. Both bodies were lying almost face down, the clothing being in order, the genitalia unharmed. The finding had in common the facts of strangulation by violence and the two cut throats. It was obvious that the two children had left the highway and gone to the dark allotments, for the detectives were able to follow the tracks of a man and two children up to the bean patch. The soft earth about the beans showed only traces of the child Lenzen's foot marks and those of the criminal: they led from the bean patch to a place some ten metres further away where the ground was much trampled, after which, for a further seven metres, at which point her body was found, the footprints of the child only were visible.

The time of the deaths can be stated very precisely as a quarter past nine. It was about that time that cries of "Mamma! Mamma!" were heard from that direction. Despite that, people passed the path close to the bean patch some moments later without noticing the bodies in the dark.

15

Case 57. The child Hamacher had bled to death where she lay from a wound in the right carotid artery, which artery was completely severed. The wound in the throat, from 13 to 7 cm. in length, was almost horizontal, the greater part being on the right side of the throat, curving upwards towards the ear. This great wound had been made by two knife cuts, one of which passed beneath the larynx, leaving a wound which gaped 5 cm., while the other severed almost completely the larynx without severing the posterior wall of it, however. The epiglottis was strongly compressed and between the epiglottis and the oesophagus on the right was haematoma almost as large as an almond. The lungs were inflated, some small quantity of blood having entered them. In the stomach I found 150 ccm. of brown-grey chyme; there was no air embolism and all organs were markedly anaemic.

Case 58. The Lenzen child also had two wounds on the right side of the throat which had penetrated only to the cutis vera. There were, besides, traces of throttling. On the right side of the throat there were typical bruises, the marks left by four finger tips. Corresponding to these marks were the two scratches under the left angle of the jaw which were curved (the throttle grip of the left hand). On the back there were four stab wounds, three on the right of the spine, one on the left those on the right had penetrated the lung and abdominal cavity; the left wound, in the seventh intercostal space, passed through the left lung up to the aorta (Plate 1). In the left pleural cavity there was 750 cc. of blood. The remarkable feature of all these wounds was their size, those on the back being tears respectively 18, 20, 25, and 30 mm. in length in the silk dress, and in the cotton underwear 18, 23, 24, and 30 mm.

These stabs lay, diagonally, from left to right. The left lung was perforated more or less horizontally near the pleura, making wounds of entry and exit 15 mm. long. The knife had then further penetrated into the aorta and left a 14 mm. horizontal wound 5 cm. under the origin of the carotid. The right lung revealed two stabs of 25 and 15 mm. and of a depth of the track of the wound 20 mm.

I quote these measurements in order to show that it is not possible to estimate accurately the breadth of the knife employed by the wounds inflicted by it.

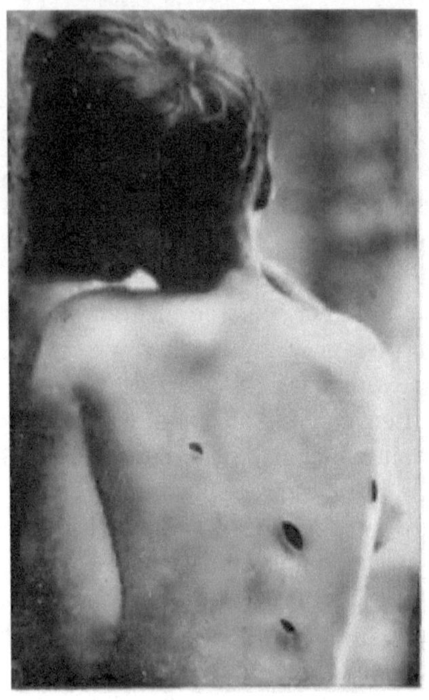

PLATE 1
KNIFE WOUNDS
(Lenzen case)

My conclusions were as follows: the true interpretation of the child murders, as the handiwork of a sadist, had to be considered as incontestable. Either they were purely lust murders, sheer killing for the sake of lustful excitement without actual sexual violation of the children; or the murderer had been disturbed and alarmed before he could consummate his purpose.

It is less easy to reconstruct the crimes themselves; though the examination of the wounds by autopsy suggests very strongly that the crimes were the work of one criminal. The absence of

17

defensive wounds on the hands of the children is evidence that they had been unconscious at the time of death. In the case of the younger girl, Hamacher, although the only external signs of injury were the throat wounds, the condition of the lungs, the compressed epiglottis and the haemorrhage into the oesophagus behind the larynx, strongly suggested strangulation. It would have been easy to use the knife in a double stroke upon a victim already unconscious. The criminal, it may be conjectured, gripped the child first and thus silenced her, next flinging her down among the runner-beans, while the other girl, now terrified, called from the allotment for her mother. The criminal must then have come up and silenced her by throttling, next cutting her throat in two attempts — the bruising being bisected by the wound suggests as much. The actual cutting of the throat was rendered difficult, it would seem, since the criminal had still to hold up his unconscious victim. Therefore, he stabbed her yet four times more in the back. At that point the girl regained consciousness and attempted to escape; but because of the stab in the aorta, she must have collapsed after a very short run.

This reconstruction of the course of events, based upon the autopsies, tallies with the clues examined upon the scene of the crime, for the footprints of the man return from the place of the struggle to the younger child, Hamacher. It must remain pure conjecture whether it was only at this point that the criminal proceeded to kill the unconscious child by cutting her throat. These child murders aroused public indignation and horror to a high degree; yet clues as to the perpetrator of the crimes were scant; indeed the foot prints and the wounds were the only available data.

The character of the lesions, both large and small, suggested the use of a sharp knife, and as the murderer used in all probability one knife only, one could deduce from the depths of the wounds the length of the weapon which inflicted them. The wound which offered the best opportunity to come at the truth in the matter was that which pierced the seventh intercostal space $3\frac{1}{2}$ cm. from the spine and penetrated up to the aorta. In the case of this particular stab the measurement is exact as the factor of uncertainty introduced where wounds have penetrated the soft parts of the body (where there may be expected a certain elasticity of the tissues) was in this case absent.

The distance from the skin surface to the aorta was ascertained as 9 cm. The dimensions of the wounds of entry were important. These were, respectively, 16, 15, and 14 mm. in lungs and aorta. It was clear that the width of the wound track was almost as wide near the aorta — 14 mm. as at the point of entry. The width uniformity of the wound track, almost to its termination, suggested to me a knife with a rather broad point. It was subsequently established that a Solingen dagger, 92 mm. in length and 19.2 mm. at its maximum width, had been used.

Case 59. On the evening of the same day a Sunday on which the bodies had been found, yet another sexual crime was discovered. The twenty-six-year-old domestic servant, Schulte, was accosted in the afternoon in Ober Cassel by an unknown man about thirty-four years of age. Schulte accompanied him and together they visited the outdoor market at Neuss, coming finally to the meadows which flank the Rhine at that part. When they had settled down the stranger, who called himself Baumgart, made immediate and importunate overtures to the girl, suggesting very plainly that there should be sexual intercourse. Using force, he held her down and attempted to remove her knickers. The girl defended herself vigorously. "I would rather die," she protested. At that moment she felt the pain of a wound in her throat and heard the words: "Then you *shall* die!" The unknown continued to stab the girl, ending with a final stab in the back so violent that the blade of the dagger broke. He then desisted, saying: "Now you can die," and made off. Hearing her cries, a party of young people came running up, found the victim still conscious, and took her at once to hospital.

The Schulte girl had three wounds on her head and neck: on the crown of her head one some 10 cm. in length; on the right ear lobe and on the front of the throat a large diagonal wound between 5 and 6 cm. in length which, however, only severed the skin and ended in a spur which suggested not one, but two movements of the blade, two distinct slashes. In addition, ten wounds were found, four of which were in pairs beginning at the left lower jaw, being 15 mm. at the point of entry, and $2\frac{1}{2}$ cm. at point of exit, somewhat lower and somewhat smaller. On the right upper arm the ulna nerve had been severed. The other six stabs were situated on the left nape of the neck (15 mm.); on the left shoulder, behind the axilla line; and on the right side between the sixth and eighth intercostal spaces penetrating into the cavity of the chest.

The last and deepest stab was that between the first and second lumbar vertebrae: from it oozed fluid; the left leg was paralysed. In the body of the first lumbar vertebra the 54 mm.-long broken piece of dagger blade was stuck. This piece of blade enabled the manufacture of the weapon to be traced to a Solingen firm. It was a weapon 92 mm. in length and 19.2 mm. wide.

The case of Schulte was of the greatest importance to the police, for here was a crime in which the criminal's method and, even more important, both man and weapon had been described minutely. Nevertheless, although this case seemed so clear it left a certain perplexity in the mind since we had formed the opinion that a sadist who had satisfied his sexual appetite on Saturday by the murder of two children would not have troubled to tackle a victim capable of offering a stout resistance already by the following Sunday. Again, strangulation, a characteristic common to all the other crimes, was here absent. But there remained the broken dagger blade to remind us, inevitably, of the knife wounds of the July victims: those wounds, obviously, might have been caused by just such a dagger.

The *German Police Journal* has commented very fully on the case of Schulte, devoting a special number to it (8th April, 1930). There the reconstructed picture of the dagger used on Schulte is reproduced. That issue has also many important photographs that are not reproduced here for lack of space.

Case 63. On Sunday, the 29th of September, 1929, the servant girl, Ida Reuter, set forth at 4 p.m. on an excursion to Düsseldorf from the place in Barmen where she was employed. The following day at 7 a.m. she was found dead in the meadows beside the Rhine, near Düsseldorf. The body was lying in a posture typical of sexual outrages, with bare legs parted, the clothing disarranged, the genitals exposed. From the site where the body was found, there were indications on the ground of its having been dragged seventy metres from a place near the promenade on the banks of the Rhine where, probably, the girl had been first attacked. The criminal had taken the knickers and the contents of her bag, the bag itself he had thrown into a garden.

When the Murder Commission arrived the body of the girl was already stiff. About the head a circle of bruises was visible. While differing as to size, some having an intricate conformation caused by successive blows on the same site, the general character of all was the same.

Plate 2 shows most of these wounds. They are surrounded by large, irregular areas of massive bruising. One notices at once the wound on the crown of the head, where the main fissure lies on an almost quadrilateral contused area. The regularity of this injury gives us, with some precision, the character of the instrument which delivered the blow.

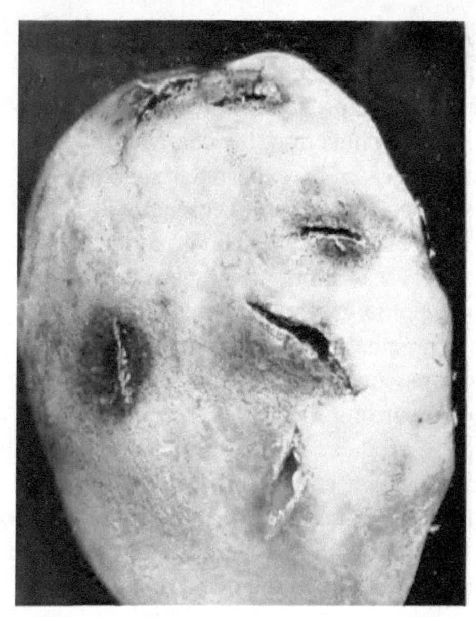

PLATE 2
HEAD HAMMER WOUNDS
(Ida Reuter case)

Although the remainder of the wounds in this Reuter case are
not surrounded by such clear and distinct squares of massive
bruising, some show the superimposition of a form roughly
square in shape, overlapping or intersecting, as it were.
From other cases we know that if a hammer strikes the skin of
the head that particular skin surface will burst in a
characteristic manner, resulting in a fissure wound more or
less gaping and a depressed fracture.
Again, it may be expected that if the surface is struck by a
direct blow, the impression of the hammer face will be left at
the point of impact. Of course, the thick hair of a young
woman would break the force of the blow and minimize the
effects of it. And it is equally obvious that if the skull is round
and the blow a glancing one, the impression will be but
partial. A point of interest I noted was the change in the
appearance of these head bruises which took place after the

parts had been preserved. For whereas, after removing the blood-clotted hair, I found them indistinct, they showed up very clearly after the process of preservation. Werkgartner mentions, in this connection, the character of wound marks in the epidermis revealed by experimental shot-gun wounds where the weapon was in direct contact with the head.

I came, therefore, to the conclusion that these head wounds, and the bruised areas about them, were the result of repeated heavy hammer blows from a square-faced hammer; for they were all in character and of a marginal length of 2 cc.

The later autopsy on the skull itself fully confirmed my first assumptions regarding it.

Before I deal with these matters I must add a little to my account of the Reuter case. On the right side of the neck, 6 cm. beneath the Eustachian tube, were three abrasions in the epidermis which, together, covered an area of from 25 mm. to 11 mm. On the left side of the neck, about a finger's breadth from the median line, was a group of minute abrasions, 47 mm. to 7 mm. in length.

The skull revealed extensive fractures of both temporal areas; on the right bigger than on the left side. Further, a chain of fractures proceeded from the squamous suture over the left side of the skull down to the battered nasal bone (compare the two upper rows of skulls in Plate 3). The brain was but little damaged. There were blood-clots in the pia mater. The dura was destroyed only superficially, 1 to 2 cm. At the base of the skull there was a fracture. There was blood in the lungs. In the stomach there was 250 cc. of chyme and food fragments mixed with blood. To go more into the details of the hole fractures of the skull needs a comparative study with the case of Dörrier, next dealt with.

Case 64. On Saturday, the 12th of October, 1929, at 6.30 a.m. the unemployed servant girl, Dörrier, was found gravely injured and unconscious. Once more the scene of the crime was in the western part of the town, namely, Flingern. As in the Reuter case, the criminal had dragged Dörrier from the scene of the crime behind some bushes. Dörrier died without recovering from the coma in which she was found, on the 13th of October. She had sustained similar, but less serious head wounds than Reuter. Round about the left temple were bruises more or less uniform and from 3 to 5 cc. long. On the right side of the head there was a large single wound of from 6 cm. to 4 cm.; and on the occiput a further wound of two parts measured 9 cm. At the entrance of the vagina there was a large tear 1 cm. by 1 cm.; in the mucous membrane were the imprints of finger nails. Both temporal muscles were lacerated and the adjoining parts of the skull splintered. On the left the dura was perforated, on the right it was torn to about 6 cm. to 4 cm. The skull showed a battering of both temples, the left from 8 cm. to 5 cm., the right, from 6 cm. to 4 cm. (Compare Plate 3.) The brain was damaged only on the surface, on the left temple there were two nut-sized wounds.

The skin wounds and the skull fractures of Reuter and Dörrier were similar to the last detail, as is shown by the skull sections of the girls (Plate 3).

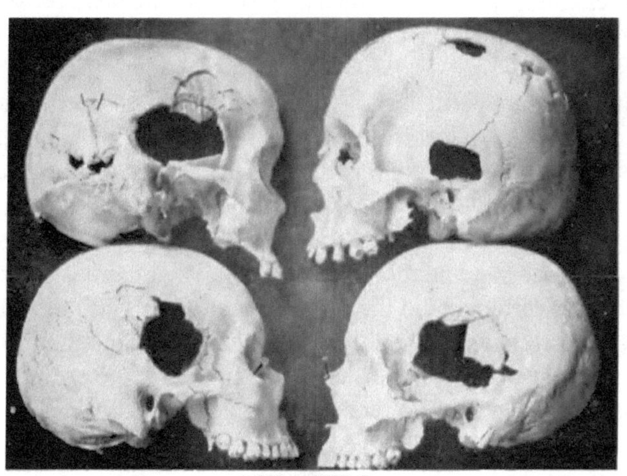

PLATE 3
SKULL HAMMER FRACTURES
(Reuter and Dörrier cases)

There you see, for example, on the right skull sections (Reuter above, Dörrier below), the same type of curved fracture extending towards the occiput, the bone fragments of which remained within the circle of the fracture. The radius of the arcs, on both cases, is almost identical. One can estimate, almost precisely, the exact number of blows which were dealt by the criminal. The two skull sections show five fractures whose edges form an outline of the hammer head.
After the comparison of the head wounds I came to the following conclusions: the wounds of Reuter and Dörrier conform to such an extent that it is necessary to presume the same criminal and the same instrument of murder in both cases. That the criminal delivered the blows with a hammer which had a convex square face of about 2 cm. The cause of death in both cases was head injuries resulting from hammer blows. It is amazing that Dörrier, whose wounds from an anatomical point of view were much more grave than those of Reuter, survived for so long. The blows on the head of Reuter were more numerous, but the injury to the brain was much less. That
Reuter died, nevertheless, so quickly was due to the injuries of the numerous vessels from which she had bled to death. The flow of blood into the lungs further accelerated death. One can sum up as follows: the blows on the head caused Reuter to fall unconscious. She had scarcely a chance to cry out. Compare this with the statement of Frau Meurer. Then there was the great loss of blood and the infiltration of blood into the lungs. Since no considerable pool of blood had been found on the promenade where the murder was committed, the criminal must have dragged Reuter away immediately after he had struck her down. He dragged her seventy metres, as was shown by the blood marks in the grass, and on arrival at that point Reuter must have been dying or already dead. Otherwise, a bigger mass of blood would have been found. In the case of both women proof of sexual violation was forthcoming. The position in which the body of Reuter was found was rather suspicious: on the back, with uncovered abdomen and widely parted legs is the typical position of the

woman who has first been silenced before being sexually assaulted.

The classification of the Reuter murder as a sexual crime explains the circumstances that the body was dragged away from the place where she was killed a promenade which is frequented by lovers after dark — to the greater solitude of the meadows beside the Rhine. There the criminal was able to commit undisturbed the sexual violation of Reuter who, it is probable, was by that time already dead.

On making an autopsy I found, when dissecting the vagina, that I was able to empty almost 2 ccm. of spermatic fluid into a glass. In the microscopic examinations which follow I found numerous spermatozoa, among them a few that still moved. These data would establish for us the hour of the crime, provided that the murder and the sexual act were committed at the same time. For this reason, the spermatozoa would have remained motile only for a few hours in the acid secretions of the vagina. The state of the digestive processes, the complete *rigor mortis* when the body was found at seven in the morning, make reasonable the assumption that the murder was committed before midnight.

In the vagina of Dörrier I was not able to establish the presence of spermatozoa. In the dissecting rooms the vagina was irrigated before being photographed because of the disagreeable odour, but the fresh tear on the posterial wall of the vaginal entrance proved that the organ had been subjected to rough treatment and thus labelled this case, too, as a sexual murder. While it is true that one cannot say with any certainty that the vaginal wound of Dörrier is a simple coitus wound, the condition revealed by the autopsy in this case does suggest the same criminal.

Case 65. On the 25th of October, 1929, Frau Meurer, thirty-four years of age, at about 8 o'clock, was on her way home along the isolated Hellweg in the Flingern district, when she was accosted by a man. "Aren't you afraid?" he said, "quite a lot of things have happened here already."

Frau Meurer paid no attention to him, but he continued to walk beside her. She cannot remember the blows which followed hard upon these words. An hour later she was brought into the hospital unconscious.

On the forehead and over the right ear the hospital physician found oval wounds of a diameter of 2 cm. with lacerated edges which exposed the bone of the scalp which was not damaged. After two weeks Frau Meurer was discharged as cured. Her wounds might have been caused by hammer blows or blows from some similar blunt instrument. This episode was important because two weeks earlier in that same place Dörrier had been killed by similar wounds. The same evening Frau Wanders was attacked in the Hofgarten in the heart of Düsseldorf. She was in the habit of soliciting there late at night and thought she had succeeded in picking up a man when she saw a stranger approaching her. After negotiating with him for a little, she received a blow on the head which rendered her unconscious. She regained consciousness very soon and went to the police and then to hospital where four head wounds were found. Later, when I made my examination, I found a square depression fracture over the left ear and two smaller depression fractures on the crown and on the right temple. They were square hammer impressions. My deduction that the wounds were the result of hammer blows was confirmed later both by the confession of Kürten and by the finding of the hammer. I shall deal later with these points in more detail.

THE LAST TWO MURDER CASES.

Case 67. On the 7th of November, 1929, Gertrud Albermann, aged five years, was seen at 7 o'clock in the evening in the Flingern district. Two days later her body was found in the morning in an isolated place against the wall of a house owned by people named Haniel. The body was lying among stinging nettles beside the footpath and was face downwards, with parted legs. The clothing appeared to be undisturbed, but on removing the coat it was seen that the clothes had been slipped up over the posterior and the knickers torn, thus exposing both posterior and perineum. The autopsy revealed little post mortem staining and anaemia, congestion of the face, and typical traces of throttling with the thumb imprints on the right. There were two stab wounds in the left side of the head, thirty-four stabs in the breast. The head stabs pierced the cranium fissures 10 and 7 mm. in length, ending in the dura. Nine stabs in the heart, three of which perforated it, five in the liver, four in and through the stomach, three in the spleen, several in the lungs (little blood breathing), two in the aorta, one penetrating. (The length of these stab wounds was 4 by 3 mm.) Three stabs in the left kindey, one in the right kidney. In the stomach 300 ccm. of coarse chyme fragments. The vagina was full of blood, the entrance being torn up to the labia majora, the anus also wounded, two wounds were on the mucous surface and the other in the sphincter. The length of the wounds at the points of entry was generally 12 mm. (9 — 16 mm.). In some of these wounds, it was plain that the knife edge had been upwards. Measurement of the wound tracts showed a maximum depth in some cases of 12 cm. for example from the surface of the breast to the posterior pleura. The body of the little Albermann child was found on the 9th of November as stated before. A few hours later the so-called "murder letter" was received: it had been posted already on the 8th of November, in the evening, in Düsseldorf, and addressed to a Communist newspaper. It contained the information that the body of the Albermann child was lying hard by the wall of the Haniels' house. Although the letter arrived too late, it became important because of a reference in it to a second body lying buried on the edge of the wood near Düsseldorf.

Once already on the 14th of October, 1929, the police had received a peculiar communication describing the interment of a body at the edge of the woods and containing a plan on which the burial place was marked. On the 15th of November, 1929, digging brought to light a female body which, by the clothing and other marks of identity, was identified as a servant girl, Maria Hahn, who had disappeared on the 11th of August, 1929.

On that day, a Sunday, Hahn had had a day off, and had last been seen in a beer-garden with a man near the place where her body was thus later found. The body of this girl, which had been lying buried for three months in the loamy earth, was quite well preserved, desiccation, the formation of adipocere, and the absence of worms had contributed to the preservation. The wounds were as follows: three stabs in the left temple, 11 — 13 mm. in length; these penetrated through the skull, that nearest the front piercing also the brain, green at that point.

In the skin of the neck there was a group of seven stabs in a small area 5 by 5 cm. These were all superficial. In the breast there were ten wounds spread over an area 22 cm. by 13 cm. The size of these punctures ranged between 9 and 11 mm., six were superficial, two penetrated the heart, two the pleurae (Plate 4). In the pericardium there was a small amount of liquid blood, and in the right pleura 250 ccm. of coagulated blood. The stomach was flaccid, containing 100 ccm. grey-yellow chyme.

The vagina was large and undamaged, the anus gaped wide, permitting the passage of three fingers, excrement and dried-up brown leaves were visible in it. The rectum was also obviously large, and when dissected was found to be 12 cm. in diameter. There were no wounds in it. Tests for spermatozoa were negative. My findings were as follows: A comparison of the autopsies of the Albermann child and Maria Hahn show a considerable affinity. Evidence of throttling could not, of course, be proved in the latter case, but the stab wounds were alike in both cases. Each body had stabs in the left temple. In the skull there were the same triangular forms showing a knife with a rather broad back. The largest stab, in the case of Hahn, was in the forehead.

On the edge of the upper end the impression of the back of the knife was quite visible, but below, instead of a sharp cutting edge there was a slight crumbling of the bone. The length was 14 mm., which shows that the blade of the knife was certainly not longer and only a little narrower. If one considers that the

29

points of entry have an average length of 12 mm., the blade
must have been about this width.

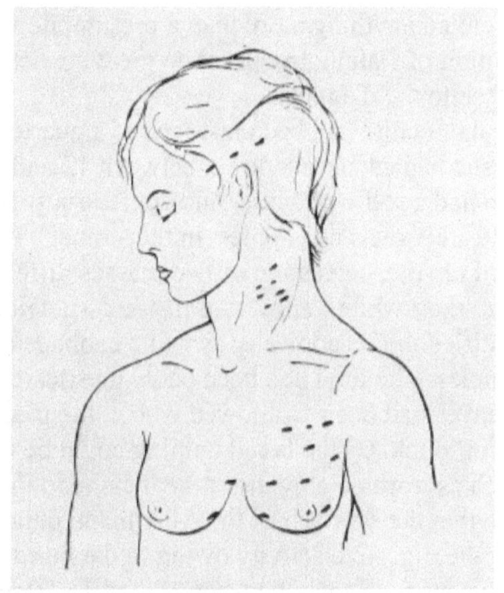

PLATE 4
SCISSOR WOUNDS
(Hahn case)

The longest wound track in the body of Albermann was 12
cm. by measurement. In coming to this conclusion, it had to
be borne in mind that the infantile breast gave way under the
weight of the stab. The wounds on the genitalia of the
Albermann child were serious, vagina and anus were torn, and
in the vagina I found spermatozoa. It follows therefore that the
vagina had been violated by forcible penetration of the penis. I
was not able to prove spermatozoa in the rectum. The anus ·
could also have been torn in the act of coitus. As far as Hahn
is concerned, there were no traces of wounds on the genitals.
The wide gaping of the anus remains obvious, even when one
considers the abnormal width of the rectum. The presence of
the dead last year's leaves suggests sexual connection with
Hahn while she was lying on the ground. The gaping of the
30

anus and the vital reaction of the sphincter muscle lead me to the conclusion of coitus per anum. Thus we have a further analogy with the case of Albermann. Even so, this conclusion cannot be called anything more than a presumption, for the decomposition of Hahn introduces too great an element of uncertainty into the diagnosis.

The Albermann child had been last seen at a quarter to 7 p.m. For lunch she had eaten sauerkraut between 12 and 1 o'clock. For tea she had a roll with butter and apple-kraut. Towards 6 o'clock she ate sweets and apples. In the stomach were 300 grammes of chyme, consisting of two masses differing distinctly in their white-yellow and rust-brown colour. The first I identified microscopically as white cabbage and the latter as apples. The food had been badly masticated, the cabbage leaves had been swallowed whole, the pieces of apple were 1-2 cm. thick. Of the bread nothing could be traced in the stomach as it was highly digestive. I came to the conclusion that the stomach of the Albermann child had stopped in the digestive activity owing to the murder, at a time when all the cabbage eaten between 12 and 1 o'clock was still in the stomach, but the roll eaten at 4 o'clock was entirely digested.

It must be borne in mind that sauerkraut is not easily digested, moreover that it had been badly chewed; a roll, on the other hand, even when swallowed in somewhat large pieces — as was the apple — may be fully digested in three hours. Hence: 4 plus 3 = 7 o'clock.

In the bowels we found neither cabbage nor apple. As the apple had been eaten at 6 o'clock and its remains were still completely in the stomach, one can arrive at the conclusion that death took place only a few hours after 6 o'clock (Hahn had less food fragments, but it is impossible to draw any useful conclusions in her case, since we do not know at what time she took her last meal). Assuming that she had a rich dinner within the hour of her death, that event had to be presumed to have occurred about midnight. The place of the death of Hahn can be presumed to have been near the place where her body was found on the edge of the wood; for it is unlikely that the murderer dragged the body very far. I have already mentioned the leaves in the anus. The body of the little Albermann was discovered in so typical a position that she must have been killed and sexually violated where she was found. The position, with widely spread legs and the clothes pulled upwards, the knickers torn up behind, arouse the inevitable suspicion that the child had been put in this position in order to rape it from behind. At the place where the body was found only the smallest traces of blood were discovered, for the rain which fell on the 7th and 8th had washed most of it away. Most of the blood had been absorbed by the clothes.

On considering the sequence of these deaths — as far as it is possible from the autopsies — one circumstance of vital importance emerges. The great lacerations in the vagina and anus bled little. The blood from this source must have been absorbed by the clothing as the child had not been undressed. But in the adjoining vest and knickers little blood was visible. Usually the tissues about the genitals which have a rich blood supply, bleed copiously. This small amount of bleeding suggests that the child was already dying at the time when it was outraged. Therefore, the sexual act must have terminated the whole course of ill-treatment. It is of importance further to note the distribution of blood on the different parts of the clothing.

The chemise, the petticoat, the vest, the frock and apron, the vicinity of the breast, the left side and the left upper back, were half drenched with blood, while the right half of the underclothing showed only a few blood spots. It would therefore follow that while the child was bleeding from the stab wounds in the breast, it must have been lying on its back and inclining to the left side. Had it been in an upright position, the blood would have run down to the legs and could not have taken the direction to the back. Upon these considerations I drew my conclusions: the criminal had throttled the Albermann child at that place where the body was found. The child had sunk down unconscious. The criminal had stabbed the child as she lay on her back through her buttoned-up coat. He unbuttoned the coat probably only to gain access to the genitals. Then he changed his mind — was he disturbed by her dying convulsions, or did he not want to put himself in contact with a victim bleeding copiously? He turned the body over on to its face, pulled the clothes up, tore the knickers and forced his penis into the vagina and anus. Then and there the child must have died. The criminal placed the coat over the uncovered abdomen of the child and thus left her lying there.

THE CLOSE OF 1929. ANALYSIS OF THE FINDINGS.

With the Albermann case the series of murders and attacks in Düsseldorf ceased. The winter remained quiet. The Düsseldorf Murderer — for such was the name the whole world had given the criminal, or criminals — had not been apprehended, despite the fact that an enormous police machine had been set in motion against him. Because of this failure the press launched an attack against the police, in my opinion, unjustly. It is only necessary to consider the facts as I have related them to appreciate how few were the clues in the hands of the police to assist them in their search for the perpetrator. Indeed, two of the attacks were perpetrated by Stausberg; the murder of Gross was at the hand of an unknown criminal; and, these three crimes apart, there remained an insufficient number of common factors upon which a theory could be constructed pointing unequivocally to a single criminal.
Where a series of crimes are committed, the same technique inevitably suggests the same criminal. That is an old aphorism of criminology. But just this very thing is missing in our cases. Certainly, there were points in common. In five murders the sexual motive was perfectly clear from the condition of the genitals. In the other cases, that of the murdered Scheer or the stabbed Kornblum, or again, in the case of Frau Meurer, it could not be definitely demonstrated. In a different category was the type of outrage that began with the strangling of the Ohliger child, Hamacher, Lenzen, and Albermann. These were cases in which throttling was a

common feature; but among the surviving victims, throttling was not employed. Further, the multiplicity of stabs in the one series of victims and the absence of stabbing in the case of the other series, along with the hammer blows, all argued against one and the same criminal. And to these factors was added the view that Stausberg had been responsible for the February attack, an opinion which held good until the November findings on Albermann. It was in particular for a criminal who dealt death with a hammer that we sought. I myself had been confirmed in this error because of my investigations of attacks which had taken place in the town of Eschweiler in the Aix la Chapelle district.

Since 1926 six attacks on women in lonely parts of the town had been reported to the police. In all these cases the criminal had approached the women unawares from behind, and rendered them unconscious with a hammer-blow to the left of the head with the object of attempting subsequent sexual outrage. On the first woman who had been attacked in 1926 I found a square depression fracture over the left ear with the length of $3\frac{1}{2}$ cm. which was already healed. The last case 30th January, 1930 had in addition lacerated bruises on the left part of the head and two cuts on the forehead and chin. The criminal from Eschweiler, obviously also a sadist, has not been identified up to now. I had presumed at once that this criminal had nothing to do with the hammer cases in Düsseldorf. Nevertheless, his technique showed similarity with one or other of the Düsseldorf cases. Thus in this case we came to the conclusion that as in the Düsseldorf case we had to assume a hammer specialist in addition to the stabber. Another grave error in the search for the principal criminal was a preconceived opinion that he must be a madman, the ghastliness of the murders, and the terror which gripped the whole population, all helped to make this error an easy one into which to fall.

One may refer here to the London killer, "Jack the Ripper," but these crimes were, after all, very different. In a short space of time, a few months, six prostitutes were murdered in Whitechapel, always in the same way, their bodies being mutilated. The London crimes stopped suddenly with the suicide of this abnormal criminal. So it was that we sought in Düsseldorf, too, for a criminal maniac.

CHAPTER II

KÜRTEN'S CONFESSIONS BRING
THE SOLUTION

Suddenly all these uncertainties and perplexities were ended by the capture of the criminal and his confession. This totally unforeseen outcome was not due to the efforts of the police, but to a sheer coincidence, coupled with the criminal's lack of caution.

It was the famous Butlies affair which resulted in the discovery. For that reason I propose to describe it here, and do so in Kürten's own words.

"On the 14th of May, 1930, I saw a man accost a young girl at the railway station and go off with her. Out of curiosity I followed the couple along the Graf-Adolf-strasse, the Karlstrasse, Klosterstrasse, Kölner Strasse, Stoffeler Strasse to the Volksgarten. When the man wanted to go into the dark park with the girl, she resisted him. I seized the opportunity and approached the couple."

"I asked him what he meant to do with the girl. He replied that the girl had no lodging and that he proposed to take her to his sister. At this point the girl asked me whether the Achenbachstrasse was in that neighborhood, it was there the man's sister was supposed to live. When I assured her very convincingly that the street was in an entirely different neighborhood, she stepped to my side, and the man made off very quickly. We returned. The girl told me that she was out of work and had nowhere to go. She agreed to come with me to my room in the Mettmanner Strasse 71. Round about 11 o'clock we got to my room which is on the third floor. Then she suddenly said she didn't want any sexual intercourse and asked me whether I couldn't find her some other place to sleep. I agreed. We went by tram to Worringerplatz and on towards the Grafenberger Wald, going along the Wolfschlucht until we came to the last of the houses. Here I seized Butlies with one hand by the neck, pressing her head back very hard and kissing her. I asked her to let me have her. I thought that under the circumstances she would agree, and my opinion was right. Afterwards I asked whether I had hurt her, which she denied. I wanted to take her back to the tram, but I did not accompany her right to it because I was afraid that she might inform the police officer who was standing there. I had no intention of killing Butlies. She had offered no resistance. We had sexual intercourse standing, after I had pulled down her knickers. There was another reason why I could not do anything to her I had been seen by a friend in the tram. I did not think that Butlies would be able to find her way back again to my apartment in the rather obscure Mettmanner Strasse. So much the more was I surprised when on Wednesday, the 21st of May, I saw Butlies again in my house."

Butlies supplements this statement thus: On the 14th of May she had come from Cologne to Düsseldorf. There on the railway station she got into contact with a "Frau Bruckner," and made an appointment with her for 8 o'clock in the evening of that day. She had then waited in vain on the railway station for the woman and in the end had been accosted by a man who wanted to put her up. Her statement corroborates Kürten's. After her adventure Butlies took the tram from the Grafenberger Wald back to the town. Then she walked the streets of Düsseldorf. At last she went to the Gertrudishaus, where she told the Sisters about the attack. On the 17th of May she wrote to her new acquaintance, Frau Bruckner, in Düsseldorf Bilker Allee a letter in which she hinted that she had fallen into the hands of a murderer. The recipient of the letter, Frau Brügmann, suspected the connection with the Düsseldorf murderer, and took the letter to the criminal police department. The writer of the letter was interrogated and eventually succeeded in finding the house of the unknown man. On her own account she had already made enquiries in different houses in the Mettmanner Strasse for a man of a certain type and, at last, she had heard from the inhabitants of No. 71 that a crying girl had once come in the same way asking for a man of the same description. Her description fitted Peter Kürten, who lodged there. That was on the 21st of May.

"On Wednesday, the 21st of May, I happened to look over the bannisters and saw Butlies and recognized her. She can be recognized easily. She has very fair hair, is slant-eyed and bow-legged. She left the house again. At lunch-time she came back. This time with a police officer. I saw her stand in the entrance door and speak to the landlady. Then in the afternoon she came again to the house, this time coming up to our floor. She entered the flat of the Wimmers and she saw me. She was startled. I think it is likely that she recognized me then. I knew what would happen after that!"

"That same evening I fetched my wife from the place where she worked: 'I must get out of the flat,' I said. I explained the Butlies case to her. But I only mentioned the attempt at sexual intercourse, saying that as it could be called 'rape,' along with my previous convictions, it was enough to get me fifteen years' penal servitude. Therefore I had to get out. I changed. Throughout the night I walked about. On Thursday, the 22nd of May, I saw my wife in the morning in the flat. I fetched my things away in a bag and rented a room in the Adlerstrasse. I slept quietly until Friday morning."

The events of this Friday were described to me by Kürten in writing.

It was at nine in the morning when I went to my flat. Shortly before I reached No. 71 two men came out of it. I found out afterwards they were detectives. I thought right away that they were that. When I went into the flat my wife was still there. When I asked her why she had not gone to work to-day she answered: 'I did, but I was taken away from it by two detectives who brought me home.' Both these men had searched the place and a few moments before they had gone down the staircase. Then my wife asked me to leave the house saying she did not want me to be arrested there. I did as she asked and later met her she had gone back to the place where she was employed. I then asked her to come with me for a little while. Two days before I had told her about the Butlies affair. To-day, the 23rd, in the morning, I told my wife that I

was also responsible for the Schulte affair, adding my usual
remark that it would mean at least ten years' or more
separation for us probably for ever. At that my wife was
inconsolable. She spoke of age, unemployment, lack of means
and starvation in old age. When the lunch hour approached I
had not even then succeeded in calming my wife down. She
raved that I should take my life. Then she would do the same,
since her future was completely without hope. Then in the late
afternoon I told my wife that I could help her. That I could
still do something for her. I told her that I was the Düsseldorf
murderer. Of course, she didn't think it possible and didn't
want to believe it. But then I disclosed everything to her,
naming myself the murderer in each case. When she asked me
how this could help her, I hinted that a high reward had been
offered for the discovery as well as for the capture of the
criminal; that she could get hold of that reward, or at least
some part of it, if she would report my confession and
denounce me to the police. Of course, it wasn't easy for me to
convince her that this ought not to be considered as treason,
but that, on the contrary, she was doing a good deed to
humanity as well as to justice. It was not until late in the
evening that she promised me to carry out my request, and
also that she would not commit suicide. I then accompanied
her almost to the door. It was 2 o'clock when we separated.
Back in my lodging I went to bed and fell asleep at once.
What happened the next morning, the 24th of May, is known.
"First a bath, then several times around the neighbourhood of
the Kortzingen's flat [Kürten had planned a robbery here].
Lunch, a hair-cut, and then, at 3 o'clock I met my wife
according to the arrangement and there the arrest took place.
As a matter of fact, my wife had carried out my order a bit too
quickly for me. I want to point out again that I never collapsed
on the 23rd or 24th of May, but kept steadily before me my
purpose to the very end."
Thus Kürten. I now contrast his statement with that of his
wife:
"In the morning, after the detectives had brought me from the
place where I work, my husband came to the flat. 'You must

have done something awful!' I said. 'Yes,' he replied. 'I did it.
I did everything.' Then, with that he left the flat. We then met
by arrangement at 11.30 in the morning in the Hofgarten. We
had dinner in a restaurant in the Duisburger Strasse. I could
not eat anything, but he ate up the lot, my portion, too."
"At 2 o'clock we were walking over the Rhine Bridge back
and forwards. In the late afternoon I asked him what he meant
with his words: 'I have done everything.' 'If you promise
solemnly that you won't give me away I'll tell you
something,' he said. I promised. 'I have done everything that
has happened here in Düsseldorf!' 'What do you mean by
that?' I asked. 'Everything — the murders and the attacks.'
'What, those innocent children, too?' I asked. 'Yes,' he said.
'Why did you do that?' I asked him. 'I don't know myself,' he
replied, 'it just came over me.'"
"Then all the big cases were talked over, including that of
Mülheim. When I got terribly excited about it all, he said,
'I've done something very silly. I ought not to have told you.'
That afternoon Kürten was very depressed and in a way I had
never seen before. He told me that he had not cried once in his
whole life, but yesterday evening, when he was alone, he had
cried bitterly. In the afternoon while we spoke only about the
fact that the detectives were after him, he was quiet and self-
possessed. But towards the evening when I wanted to go home
he was as I have never seen him in his life before. He was
very cast down. He could not look into my eyes. All the
indifference had disappeared. He burst out with it all, telling
of the murders and the attacks as if some power forced him to
it. I thought he had gone crazy. Nothing had been said about
any reward."
Who could not understand Frau Kürten who would reproach
her that she was not able to carry alone the weight of this
ghastly secret but that she gave it away to the police when
pressed by them? She had a last meeting with her husband
near the Rochus Church, for the following day, the 24th. That,
too, the woman, who was quite distraught, reported to the
police. The church square was quietly surrounded and Kürten
was arrested as he walked towards his wife. He was quite

composed. Subsequently, he often told me how he smilingly calmed the detective who advanced excitedly towards him, the revolver levelled at him.

When Kürten was questioned by the police he not only told of the attacks of 1929, but he gave also an account of a long chain of crimes without being questioned. For reasons to which I will return presently he lengthened this chain with some imaginary links, but he soon brought it back again to the facts.

TABLE I

THE SEQUENCE OF THE CRIMES
ACCORDING TO KÜRTEN'S OWN STATEMENT

Born 1883 in Köln-Mülheim. Passed his childhood there. Left for Düsseldorf 1894; 1897 apprenticed as a moulder. In 1899 first convicted for theft.

TABLE OF OFFENCES

Nov. 1899 Attempted strangulation   18-year-old girl unknown.

FROM 1900 TO 1904 IN PRISON

1904	Arson	Barn after harvest.
1904	Arson	Hay loft.
1904	Arson	Two hay-ricks.

1905 to 1913 IN PRISON

1913	Attempted strangulation	Margarete Schäfer.
1913	Murder by strangulation and throat-cutting.	Christine Klein, Mülheim.
1913	Axe blow	Unknown man
1913	Axe blow	Unknown woman.
1913	Axe blow attempt	Hermes, sleeping girl.
1913	Strangulation	Gertrud Franken
1913	Arson	Hay-rick and hay wagon.

1921	Strangulation	War widow.
1925	Strangulation	Tiede.
1925	Strangulation	Mech.
1925	Strangulation	Kiefer.
1926	Strangulation	Wack.
1927	Arson	Three hay-ricks.
1927	Arson	Shock of sheaves.
1927	Arson	Two barns.
1927	Attempted strangulation	Anni Ist.
1927	Arson	Two barns.
1927	Arson	Plantation.
1928	Arson	Barn.
1928	Arson	Farmyard.
1928	Arson	Shock of sheaves (twice).
1928	Arson	Hay-rick.
1928	Arson	Hay wagon.
1928	Arson	House.
1928	Arson	House.
1928	Arson	Shed.
1928	Arson	Forest fire.
1928	Arson	Haystacks.
1928	Arson	Sheds.
1929	Arson	Stacks.
1929	Arson	Barns, sheds, stacks, (ten cases).

1929

Feb. 3	Attack with scissors	Frau Kühn.
Feb. 13	Stabbed and killed	Rudolf Scheer.
March. 8	Strangled and stabbed after death	Child— Rose Ohliger
March	Attempted, strangulation	Edit Boukorn.
July	Attempted strangulation	Maria Witt.
July	Attempted strangulation	Maria Mass.
July	Attempted strangulation	Unknown domestic servant.
August	Strangled and stabbed to death	Maria Hahn
August	Strangled and drowned	"Anni," a housemaid.
August	Stabbed with dagger	Anna Goldhausen.
August	Stabbed with dagger	Frau Mantel.
August	Stabbed with dagger	Kornblum.

August	Strangled and throat cut	Child—Hamachner.
August	Strangled and stabbed	Child—Lenzen.
August	Stabbed with dagger	Gertrud Schulte.
August	Attempted strangulation and thrown into river	Heer.
Sept.	Blow with tool	Rück.
Sept.	Attempted strangulation	Maria Rad.
Sept.	Killed by hammer blows	Ida Reuter.
October	Killed by hammer blows	Elisabeth Dörrier
October	Attack with hammer	Frau Meurer.
October	Attack with hammer	Frau Wanders.
November	Strangled and stabbed with scissors	Child Albermann.

1930

February	Attempted strangulation	Hilde.
March	Attempted strangulation	Marianne Dal Santo.
March	Attempted strangulation	Irma.
April	Attempted strangulation	Sibille.
April	Attempted strangulation	Unknown girl from Herne.
April	Attempted strangulation	Young woman, Hau.
April	Attacks	Several girls.
April	Attack with hammer	Charlotte Ulrich.
May	Attempted strangulation	Maria Butlies.
May	Attempted murder	Gertrud Bell.

The way in which Kürten enumerated all his offences, tabulated here in a sequence chronologically accurate, and the way in which he dictated it with every detail, is quite extraordinary. He was not accused of these crimes one by one, but reeled off on his own account, beginning with No. 1 and ending with No. 79, every single case, dictating them, in fact, to the stenographer and even showing enjoyment at the horrified faces of the many police officers who listened to his recital, day by day. Kürten was examined very closely by the Criminal Investigation Department and by the judge. Even so, I got him to describe to me personally the precise details of all the cases. A comparison of my shorthand note with the protocol of the police and judge shows a close similarity on all main points of fact. His statements show his character, his

43

intelligence, his instinctual life, so clearly that from it every reader educated in criminal psychology can obtain an absolutely clear picture of the personality of the criminal. Therefore I propose to record not only his talk concerning the cases of 1929 which are, of course, of great interest, but also these other cases. From his recital of the facts it transpires that my original deductions set forth earlier in this work were correct.

The following is the original form of Kürten's statement. As I propose to deal with the motives, as he gave them to me, in a later chapter, I shall not touch upon them at the moment. I might mention here the fact that Kürten, when interrogated by the police officers, suppressed facts, or misrepresented them in order not to disclose the motive that actuated him. In the following cases the numbers are those of the above table.

CASE 1. THE FIRST MURDER.

Kürten gave the following statement: "In November 1899 I picked up an eighteen-year-old girl in the Alleestrasse. I went with her to the Hofgarten, past the Zoo, to the Grafenberger Wald as far as Rolandsburg. On the way home amid lovely country I throttled her. I left her lying there, supposing her to be dead and heard no more of her."

Nothing could be discovered concerning this case which went back thirty years. Note how exactly Kürten remembers all the details of his work.

CASE 6. MARGARETE SCHÄFER.

This case is interesting because the statement of Kürten can be compared with the statement of the throttled victim.

Kürten thus describes the affair: "In June 1913 I picked up a girl on the Brehm strasse and took her out on several subsequent occasions. One Sunday we went to a dance at Gerresheim. On the way home I throttled the girl several times. When she was scared I said: 'That's what love's like. I won't kill you, though.' After that she put up with it. We had sexual connection on a bench."

To the jury Margarete described her adventure with Kürten as follows: "We walked in the woods the whole night. Kürten would not let me go home. He had my bag with the keys in it. He wanted to kiss me and he knocked me about, afterwards becoming friendly again. Then he threw me on to a bench and tried to have sexual intercourse with me. In the struggle my dress got torn and I cried, and then he became kinder again. I looked simply awful and in that state could not have taken the tram. We sat on a bench. Kürten threw his coat about us both and we fell asleep. Dawn came and I woke him up. Then he started again as before, tore off my ear-rings, bit me, half strangled me, pulling my hair out in handfuls. He looked like the very devil himself. I begged him to calm down for otherwise he would end in hell. My words had some effect and he did calm down. He made me swear that I would not tell anything to anybody we might meet. We came eventually to the Rolandsburg. Kürten had breakfast there. I went to the waiters who were sitting in another room and told them of the jam I was in."

CASE 7. MURDER OF THE CHILD KLEIN.

It was about the same time, in the summer of 1913, that there took place a strangling case that was not equalled in ghastliness until the year 1929. It was Kürten's first murder. Kürten thus describes it:

"In the summer of 1913 I committed many thefts. It was my speciality to frequent at such times houses where the ground floors were utilized as business premises, in particular, inns, where the proprietor and his family lived above."

"It was easy to search such premises without fear of discovery. For this purpose I have even left Düsseldorf and gone to other towns. I went to Cologne, and, in particular, to Köln-Mülheim, the town which is, by the way, the town of my birth."

"One Sunday evening it was a Feast day I searched for a suitable house and came at length to the Wolfstrasse. I broke into a house in this street, an inn owned by Klein. I went up to the first floor. This was about 10 or 11 o'clock. I opened different doors but found nothing worth stealing. In a room facing the stairs there was a bed in the left corner near the window where I entered. It was a large bed in which adults could sleep. In the room were also a cupboard and a table. "So much light came through the window from the street that I could see clearly everything in the room. In the bed I saw a sleeping girl of about ten, covered with a thick feather bed. She was lying with her head towards the window. I seized her by the neck with my hands and throttled her for one or two minutes. The child woke up, struggled to free herself, scratched my hand and then became unconscious and still." "Her arms were thrown up above her head. I then drew her head over the edge of the bed and threw the feather bed to the foot of it. With one or two fingers I penetrated the genitals. With a small but sharp pocket knife I made a deep cut in the throat of the child. I started on the left side of the throat, drawing the knife to the right with the right hand. I heard the blood gurgle up and drip on the mat. It spattered my hand. The whole business did not take more than three minutes. I then left the room and made off."

How very clearly, after seventeen years, Kürten remembered every detail of the place and of the crime, a comparison with the photograph of this room in the Public Prosecutor's Department at Düsseldorf shows.

The autopsy revealed the following:

The 111 cm. long corpse was pallid. There was hardly any post mortem staining. On the face there were regular blue-red ecchymoses. The tongue was bitten. On the throat there were two wounds separated from each other, the one shallow, only 1 to 2 mm. deep, the other deep, 9 cm. in length. The upper wound edge suggested a single stroke, the lower wound had been made by four movements. The pathologist thus describes the four cuts. One between the annular and thyroid cartilage, one deeper through the thyroid cartilage to the oesophagus.

On the skin of the neck about the throat the marks of scratches and nail imprints. The perineum was torn from vagina to rectum, several tears extending to the mucous membrane of the upper vaginal passage. It is a noteworthy fact also that the bronchial tubes were filled with blood and that both carotids were undamaged. In the stomach there was 100 ccm. of chyme.

Certain discrepancies in the autopsy show that the memory of Kürten, otherwise extremely good, becomes unreliable at the climax of the sadistic gratification (i.e., four knife wounds instead of one, the different position of the body). After the murder in Mülheim there followed those incendiary crimes which are rather regularly distributed throughout the career of Kürten. Kürten also alleges that he attacked two people with an axe from behind about that time. But as these alleged crimes were committed seventeen years ago it was impossible to trace them. Nevertheless, I mention them here because of the circumstantial account of them given by Kürten.

CASE 8.

"One Saturday evening in June, 1913, I left home at 8 o'clock and set out for Gerresheim. From a cellar under the Holy Trinity Church I took a chopper. At about 11 o'clock I saw an unaccompanied girl enter a house. In the passage I gave her a sharp and heavy blow on the head so that she crumpled up without a murmur. The girl was about 1.68 m. tall, slim, and between eighteen and twenty years of age."

CASE 9.

"In July 1913 I went with a chopper to Gerresheim about 9 o'clock in the evening. After a long search I saw a man sitting on a bench in the park. I crept up to him and hit him on the head and he collapsed without a sound. On my way back I set fire to a cart laden with hay." With the following attempt the short chopper period is finished.

47

CASE 10.

"In July 1913 I went up to the first floor of the house on the corner of the Münster and Ulmenstrasse. I had a chopper with me. I had been to the house once already to steal. I was just about to cleave through the head of the sixteen-year-old girl when a man jumped out of bed. I ran away, throwing the chopper on the bed as I ran."
(Witnesses corroborate this statement. When the householder came home after chasing Kürten in vain, he found the chopper on the blanket of his child's bed.)
Here I want to observe that Kürten dared to approach men on three occasions only. In one case the man had fallen asleep, and in the other two they were, or appeared to be, drunk. These were cases 9, 47, and 56. Kürten's precautions were so great that he even desisted from his attack upon a woman victim if she only had firmness enough to offer a courageous resistance.

CASE 11. GERTRUD FRANKEN.

"At about 9 o'clock in the evening on a Saturday in July, 1913, I set out for the house of the Loscheckes. I had a skeleton key with me and with it gained entrance to the first floor. I went into a room and up to the bed and strangled one of the children lying in it for some time. I left the room and went home again. There were three beds in the room. The girl I throttled was, I reckon, sixteen or seventeen years old. She did not scream or shout."
The strangled girl was born in 1896 thus Kürten had estimated her age correctly. A big interval now follows in the sequence of the crimes, due to a long term of penal servitude followed by Kürten's marriage in Altenburg. Then, once more, in the environs of Düsseldorf, a place well known to him, Kürten renewed his criminal activities.

CASE 14.

In 1925 Kürten started to have relations with two servant girls, Tiede and Mech. This is how Kürten tells of it: "I met Tiede and had sexual relations with her in her room where she was employed in the Bodinus strasse. I got something good to eat there, too, and I could do with it, for I had at that time to work pretty hard. A week after meeting Tiede, I became acquainted with Mech, a housemaid in a situation on the Bergischen Landstrasse. There, too, I got something to eat. I often grabbed Tiede by the throat and seized hold of her. When she got angry with me I used to try and pacify her. 'That's what love means' I told her. She let herself be calmed down. I had not told her my real name and I had pretended to be younger by ten years, and that I had a better job than I really had. Then my wife came along and Tiede realized that I was married and gave me away to the police. I got two months' imprisonment for attempted seduction. During the trial I defended myself vigorously against the charge. But I got the two months and did it, in 1927."

"Then Mech and Tiede met and Mech cut up rough and charged me with rape, but I was acquitted. Then she charged me with using threats and insulting behaviour. For that I got eight months' imprisonment. I served six months, two being remitted on my undertaking to leave Düsseldorf. That wasn't so easy, so I wrote to the Ministry with the result that the condition was cancelled." Next follow several cases of strangling.

CASE 16. MARIA KIEFER.

"In the summer of 1925 I picked up Maria Kiefer in the Parkstrasse. We made an appointment for the following evening. I went to her place as agreed upon and there Kiefer waited for me at the front door. That was about 10 o'clock. She took me with her into the washhouse in the cellar where we had sexual intercourse, but not without her consent. Then I seized her by the throat and strangled her, but Kiefer managed to escape from the grip of my hands and cried out. So I left the house quickly."

Investigations revealed that Kiefer was born in 1889 and died in 1929, but to a witness she had told how she had been accosted by a man who she learnt later was married.

CASE 17. MARIA WACK.

"In the spring of 1926 I picked up Maria Wack in the Duisburgerstrasse. We went into the Hofgarten and talked about our personal affairs."

"We met frequently after that and one Sunday we went to the Grafenberger Wald. There I attempted to force her backwards on a bench while I seized her throat. As she put up a resistance I abandoned the attempt and left her on the bench. I never saw her again."

Wack comments upon this as follows: "In June 1926 I became acquainted with a man who called himself Fritz Ketteler. I was cleaning the doorstep when he accosted me. We made an appointment and inside three weeks we had been out five times. Ketteler was an employee of the railway and behaved decently in every way. One Sunday he suggested that we should go to the Grafenberg. Dusk had fallen in the woods and we were passing a bench when he suddenly seized me, flung me on it and groped with his hand under my skirt. I defended myself. Apparently, passers-by frightened him, for he desisted. I jumped up, grabbed his hat, and ran away. He called after me, asking for his hat. He then exchanged his hat for mine and made the remark that I ought to be human. There he left me standing, and made off."

CASE 22. ANNIE IST.

"In the summer of 1927 I picked up a girl named Annie Ist on the Brehmstrasse. From then on I saw her frequently. On a Saturday evening we went into the Grafenberger Wald. We had sexual intercourse on a bench. I then seized Ist's neck and strangled her. But she was a robust girl and managed to free herself. She ran away screaming. Her dress had been torn at the neck."

Ist comments as follows: "Kürten's statement is correct. He called himself Ketteler, Mettmanner Strasse 71. We met each other several times. On one occasion it ended with sexual intercourse. At the end of July, 1927, we went to a fair at Rath and returned through the Grafenberger Wald. It was there that we had sexual relations, but when Kürten wanted intercourse a second time I demurred, but at last gave in. After intercourse, he strangled me without any reason, bashed my face and tore my dress from my neck. Nevertheless, I asked him to take me home, which he did. We met each other several times again, but there were no more sexual relations. I got some information about him and discovered that his name was not Ketteler, and that he was a married man, so I broke off our relationship. When I saw in the newspapers the photograph of the Düsseldorf murderer, I recognized him instantly, but I did not denounce him to the police." Now I come to the cases of 1929.

CASE 45. FRAU KÜHN. 3.2.29

Kürten states as follows: "On a Sunday evening I strolled about the neighborhood of the Hellweg in search of a victim. I had pocketed a pair of scissors for this purpose. Towards 6 o'clock I saw a woman, going along the Bertastrasse. I went up to her and shouted 'Stop!' and then 'No noise!' Then with the scissors I stabbed her blindly. I left her lying unconscious. I heard cries for help and made my way quickly down the Hellweg. When I was cleaning the scissors at home I noticed that from one blade the pointed part had been broken off about 8 to 10 mm. I had thought that the stabs were much deeper." (By X-ray photograph I was able to determine the fact that the point of the scissors was impacted in the bone. When Frau Kühn was confronted by Kürten she failed to recognize him because of the darkness at the time of the attack.)

CASE 46. THE MURDER OF THE OHLIGER CHILD.

Kürten's account: "On the 8th of February, 1929, I left home
at about 6 o'clock at night. I went towards St Vincent's
Church where I met a girl between eight and ten years of age.
I asked her where she wanted to go. She said: 'Home.' I
asked, 'Where do you live?' She said: 'In the Langerstrasse.' I
said: 'Come, then, I'll take you home.' I took her by the hand
and led her along the Kettwiger Strasse as far as a hoarding.
Here I seized the child's throat, strangled her and put her on
her back. With my right hand I drew the scissors out and
stabbed the child in the left temple and in different places
about the heart. The child seemed to be dead. I went back to
my flat and searched myself for blood stains. I also cleaned
the scissors. There were no blood stains on my clothing. Then
I went to the movies as I still had a free ticket, and then home
again. I filled a beer bottle with petroleum we have a
petroleum lamp and then went to the scene of the crime with
the object of pouring it over the body and setting fire to it. But
there were too many people about. I therefore leant the bottle
against the hoarding and went home. The next morning, at 6
o'clock, I got up and told my wife I had to go to the W.C. I
ran quickly to the scene of the crime, poured the petroleum
over the body and set it on fire. There and back did not take
me more than five or six minutes. I felt no sexual excitement
and did not touch the girl. My motive was only to cause
excitement and indignation. I wanted to increase the general
indignation by setting light to the victim."
"I did not masturbate on the corpse, nor did I even touch the
child sexually. The place where I first throttled and stabbed
the child is only one or two metres from where I put her
down. When I strangled her she was standing. I took two or
three paces with her towards the hoarding. I had both hands
on her neck and dragged her with her feet on the ground."
(When the child was dragged one of her shoes slipped off and
was later found at that place.)

CASE 47. SCHEER.

"On the 12th of February, 1929, I left home about 8 o'clock in the evening and for three hours I searched in vain for a victim. My wife, I knew, would be returning home about 1 o'clock. Then in the Hellweg I ran into a man. He seemed to be drunk and noisy. He shoved me. 'What do you want?' he asked. I looked at his hands to see whether he was armed. Then with the flat of my hand I struck him in the neck. He went over backwards and fell flat on his face. I took the scissors and gave him a heavy stab with them. He grabbed for my legs and half lying, half kneeling, in front of me, clung to me. I next stabbed him in the right temple and again in the neck. At one stab in the back my scissors stuck and I could hardly get them out again. After another stab in the back I heard the blood spouting. Scheer collapsed. He relaxed his hold on my leg and lay face downwards. Even in the dark I could see the large pool of blood. I grabbed his feet and dragged him towards the ditch and shoved him until he rolled down. After that I wanted to go home, but after taking thirty steps or so I turned back and cleaned the uppers of Scheer's boots to obliterate the traces of my finger prints. The whole thing didn't take me more than eight minutes, one of which I spent standing over Scheer before I dragged him to the ditch. Next day, at 8 o'clock, I returned to the scene of the crime. On my way back I met a detective and opened a conversation with him. He, too, probably was going to the place where the murder had been committed, for detectives were already standing there. The detective looked at me suspiciously. How had I come to know of the crime? he enquired. I told him I had heard of it by telephone. Meanwhile we had come to the cordon and I was stopped." (This fantastic episode was later confirmed during the hearing by the detective in question. I wonder what would have been the result had the detective been as clever and quick in sizing up the situation as was Kürten.) The following cases, 49 to 51 and 53, are again cases of strangling.

CASE 49. MARIA WITT.

The tragi-comedy of the 11th of July, 1929, Kürten described
as follows at the police station investigation: "During the first
half of July, 1929, I picked up a servant girl named Maria
Witt on the Grunerstrasse. We chatted pleasantly and made an
appointment. Several times we met in the Heinrichstrasse.
One Sunday I fetched her to go to Kaiserswerth. Suddenly on
the Graf-Recke-Strasse my wife came up from behind us with
the words: 'Ha, ha! So you've got yourself a new wife, have
you?' With a rose that Maria had brought me from the garden
of her employer, I gave my wife a smack on the cheek. Then,
without a single word, I turned and left both the women
standing there. The scissors I had put in my pocket."
Maria Witt confirms this statement: Kürten had introduced
himself as Ketteler, a locksmith, entitled to a pension, being in
the employment of a gas company. She had a good impression
of him and had on one occasion actually sent roses to his
supposititious address on the Ackerstrasse. "His wife came up
to us with the words: 'Oh, how nice!' and struck me in the
face with her hand."

CASE 50. MARIA MAAS. 21 JULY, 1929.

"That Sunday after I had left my wife and Maria Witt, I
picked up another girl and asked her to come with me to the
Heerdter Festival. We remained there for some time. I bought
some peaches and then we strolled towards the Rhine. We sat
there and talked, meanwhile dusk had fallen. Suddenly, I
gripped her neck and strangled her violently, but she freed
herself and ran into a tent nearby." Maas, who was born in
1904, made this statement: "When the man accosted me and
introduced himself, I only caught his Christian name Fritz and
that he was a Post Office official. He behaved in every way
like a gentleman. We went to the Festival and there he bought
peaches. We also went to a beer garden, and afterwards we
strolled towards the Rhine. He asked me repeatedly for a kiss,
but when it darkened I wanted to go home. On that he gripped

my neck and without a word compressed it. I freed myself and ran towards a little tent. For days five impressions of the nails of his hand were visible on my neck." The girl, by the way, did not report to the police voluntarily: she had to be searched for.

CASE 53. ANNI.

"On the same evening I picked up a girl on the Oberkasseler Brucke who called herself Anni. We went to a beer garden. Anni said that she came from Westphalia. When darkness fell I strangled her throat until I thought she was dead. Then I dragged her along the bank and threw her into the Rhine." This case could not be traced or cleared up. No girl had been reported missing and as it is a very rare thing that a body thrown in the Rhine does not come up again, the police doubt the truth of Kürten's statement.

CASE 51.

The girl in the Freitagstrasse Kürten alleges he met between the 21st and 28th of August, 1929. He did not know the name. He had taken her for a walk along the banks of the Rhine to see the firework display. Then when he attempted to throttle her she had run away screaming. This case could not be traced.

CASE 52. THE HAHN CASE.

No other crime is more significant for an understanding of the personality of Kürten than this. Kürten himself has told about it in all its details, and even confessed to the examining magistrate the sexual motive. Here is his statement: "On the 8th of August, 1929, I was strolling in the Zoo district. I hadn't any intention of committing any offence on a girl at the time. On the Hansaplatz a girl was sitting on a bench. She accosted me. I sat down beside her and we talked pleasantly together and made a date for an excursion to the Neanderthal the next Sunday. On Sunday, punctually at 1.30 in the afternoon, I found myself in the Hansaplatz where the girl was already waiting. We went to the Neanderthal, visited a beer garden and then on to the Stinter mill. We stayed there for three hours, drank a glass of red wine each. There also I bought her a slab of chocolate. Towards 7 o'clock we went to Erkrath where we had supper with beer. We then strolled past the house of the Morps, and along by the river. Here we decided to have sexual intercourse. After sexual intercourse we left the bank of the river and went into the meadow. Here I decided to kill her. I led Hahn to a big bush near a ditch and there we settled down. It was half past nine. Suddenly I strangled her until she became unconscious, but she came to herself quickly again. Again I strangled her. After a bit I stabbed her in the throat with the scissors. She lost a lot of blood but regained consciousness, repeatedly asking me in a feeble voice to spare her life. I stabbed her in the breast a blow that probably pierced the heart. I then gave her repeated stabs in the breast and head. The process of dying probably took an hour. I let the body roll into the ditch and threw branches over it. Then I crossed the meadow and came to the road that runs from Morp-Papendell highway. I had taken the handbag of Hahn with me. From it I took the watch of the dead girl. I made a gift of it to somebody later on. The bag with the keys I threw into an oatfield."

"When I got home my wife was already in bed. Next morning we had a row, because she was suspicious about the night before. She became so excited about it that I made up my mind that I would have to find some way of seeing that the body of Hahn wasn't discovered, otherwise my wife would connect the blood stains on my clothes with it. So I went again on Monday after finishing work to the scene of the crime and pondered where I could bury the body. I went back to the flat and fetched a shovel, inventing an excuse to give my wife. Near the scene of the crime, in the corner of the wood, I dug a deep hole in a fallow field, and carried the body along the footpath, avoiding the oatfield. By the hole I put the body down. I got into the hole and dragged the body down to me. Here I laid it on its back as one buries a body. A shoe had slipped off when the body was dragged down and I laid it

beside it. Then I filled the hole. During the whole of this funeral ceremony a sentimental feeling possessed me. I caressed the hair and the first shovelful of earth I strewed thinly and gently on the body. I stamped the earth down and smoothed the soil as it was before. As my shirt had become bloody in carrying the body I took it off and washed it in the river and put it on again still wet. I hid the shovel near the river, then I went home and arrived there about 6 o'clock. My wife began reproaching me, asked me where I had been wandering all the night. I had cleaned my shoes thoroughly in the grass, using a cleaning rag which I always carried with me. I then drank coffee and went to work in the same clothes. After I had put the body of Hahn in the grave I removed her wrist-watch. Four weeks later I gave the watch to Kaete W... W... lives in the same house where I live. She often came into my room and we repeatedly had sexual intercourse."
(The witness W... vehemently denied this assertion. I found, as a matter of fact, that she was a virgin with enlarged introitus of the vagina.)
The shovel was in fact found at the place indicated. Frau Kürten confirms the hour at which her husband left her on the 12th of August, namely, about 11 o'clock p.m., when he gave as explanation that he was on night work. Between 5 and 6 o'clock he had come back with dirty shoes and blood on his clothes. Later Kürten admitted that he had not given the wrist watch to the witness W... The first assertion that he had done so was an act of vengeance for the trouble she had given him and the part she had taken in bringing about his capture. Because he had seen her the day before his arrest with Butlies, he drew this conclusion.
Now Kürten changed the instrument of murder and used a dagger instead of scissors.

CASE 54.

"On the day of the Coronation Ball, at the Lierenfelder Festival, I worked overtime until 10 p.m. I went to the Schützenplatz on the Erkrather Strasse in search of a victim. I watched the young girls, how they went home in different directions. I followed two and presently they stopped before a street door. I passed them thinking that one would probably go on. I crossed to the other side of the street and saw that one girl had gone on. I went back again to the other side of the street, keeping my dagger in readiness. I stabbed the girl in the left breast. It was the girl Goldhausen. She collapsed without a sound. I then went off with the dagger unsheathed. I heard cries for help."

CASE 55.

"When I went down the Erkrather Strasse I saw a woman coming along. I offered her my company. The woman did not answer, but crossed the road. I followed her and stabbed her twice in the back from behind."

CASE 56.

"I then went across the field path. I saw a man lying in a ditch and just about to crawl up the bank. I gave him a stab in the back. I sheathed the dagger and hid it near the Erkrather Strasse. I watched how the physician and ambulance arrived and how a crowd of curious people gathered round. I pictured to myself the indignation of the population, and then went home. It was half past two."

Three days later followed the murders of the children in Flehe: 24th August, 1929.

CASE 57.

"On the 24th of August I went out about 8 o'clock and took the dagger with me. I had heard that the Festival was on in Flehe. Until 10 o'clock I was on the look-out for a victim on the streets of Flehe. I saw two girls. They went down a field path. I followed them and told the bigger girl to fetch me from a kiosk four cigarettes for twenty pfennig. She ran off and I stayed behind with the smaller girl. I seized her by the throat, took her over my arm and carried her across the field to another small field path, where beans grew."
"Here I put down the Hamacher child, who was now unconscious, drew my dagger from my pocket and slit her throat. I stood over the body of the child with my legs apart and cut from my left to the right. I returned the dagger to the sheath. Put the sheath into my hip pocket."

CASE 58.

"I went back to the place where Lenzen, the bigger girl, had left us. She gave me the cigarettes. I seized her by the throat and strangled her. With my left arm I seized her round the body and carried her, still throttling her, down the path, round the bean patch to the garden, so that I was hidden by the beans. I loosened my right hand. Lenzen slumped down. I realized that she was not quite unconscious. She moved about and began to scream. I then seized her throat with my left hand and holding her down like that, I drew the dagger from my pocket with my right hand and in that position I stabbed her in the breast and side. I then relaxed my grip. Lenzen sank to the ground. Then I made off and at half past eleven I was home again. My wife was still awake. We talked quite naturally. There were no blood stains on me. Neither were my hands bloody. On the way home I had cleaned my dagger with a rag I found. If Lenzen was found in some other position, then she must have moved of her own volition. I left her lying on her back. On the way to the scene of the crime she defended herself vigorously, lashing out with hands and feet.

59

On the following Sunday, the 25th of August, I went once more to Flehe to savour the effect of my crime. I listened to the various accounts given by the inhabitants, going from group to group of excited people, listening to them. It gave me pleasure that the lovely bright Sunday in Düsseldorf had been shattered as by a lightning stroke."

CASE 59.

Twenty-four hours after the murder of the children, the attack on Schulte took place. This case is extremely important, because it enables us to compare Kürten's confession with the statement of the witness.

Kürten said: "Just about that time my obsession was rather strong upon me. Feeling fairly sure that I would be successful in finding a victim on that day, I had pocketed my dagger. I crossed the Rhine bridge to Oberkassel and there accosted a young girl. Together we went to Neuss where the fair was in progress. I suggested that we should take the path across the Rhine meadows on the homeward way. As we went along we repeatedly embraced and kissed each other. We sat down near the Rhine and I caressed her, but she refused me sexual intercourse. I knelt beside her, caressed with my left hand her hair, then I seized my dagger with my right hand and attempted to cut her throat. She shouted out loudly and struggled hard. Then blindly I went on stabbing her. Her shouts, however, attracted people, who called out, 'what's the matter?'"

"I went off, but remained standing in a ditch near by, and so saw how Schulte was found by some people. I went quietly over the dam to the Rhine bridge. I could still hear them calling: 'Quick! Police!' At the last stab I had noticed that my dagger was broken, therefore I threw it away. In Oberkassel I took Schulte's bag from my breast pocket, took out the watch and a picture and threw the bag in a garden. Sitting on a bench I awaited the arrival of the police. I was curious to know how much time would elapse before they arrived. Some twenty minutes passed and the thought of the police busy with my victim relieved my tension. I thought that certainly Schulte would die of her wounds. Under the bright light of the street lamp, I examined my clothes for blood, and then I went home. There was no blood on me."

The twenty-seven-year-old Gertrud Schulte said, contradicting him: "Kürten had been decent to the very end. There was no talk of kissing until after we had settled down. Then he tried to pull off my knickers and threw me backwards. This tussle did not last more than two minutes. He suddenly released me, held me by one hand and said: 'Come! See if you can feel it. I've only a small tail.' Then he threw himself on top of me and knelt between my legs. I threatened to scream. He said: 'You can shout here as much as you like. Nobody will hear you.' Obviously, Kürten had not noticed a tent nearby. He laughed when I said: 'Let me die!' 'Then you shall die!' he replied. I felt a cut on my throat and shrieked. I felt another painful stab in my back and then became unconscious." Between these dagger attacks and the hammer attacks which began soon afterwards, three minor attacks were perpetrated.

CASE 60.

Lina Heer. "It was on a Saturday, and I picked up a girl on the railway station. We went to Schumacher's and drank a glass of beer, and then walked in the Hofgarten until one o'clock in the morning. Lina seemed prepared to go home with me. As the last train had gone we went along the banks of the Düssel, through Flingern to the Ostpark. There I seized Lina's throat and strangled her. She defended herself stoutly, at which I released her again. But I strangled her again and at last pushed her into the Düssel." On that Lina comments: "I met a man who promised to find some 'digs' for me. On the banks of the Düssel he tried to rape me. When he did not succeed he pushed me in the Düssel. I only just managed to save myself."

CASE 61. SOFIE RÜCK.

"In the autumn of 1929, I met a couple in the Rossstrasse. I wanted to interfere, so I hit the man over the head with a chisel. The man ran away. Then I hit the girl several times with the chisel. She fell down. I went off." Sofie Rück, in contradiction, said: "I was cycling on the Rossstrasse. From a side street a man rushed out, dragged me off my bicycle and hit me on the head. For a short while I was unconscious. Then people came. It was on the 31st of August, 1929, at 10 o'clock. I was most certainly alone."

CASE 62. MARIA RAD. 26 SEPTEMBER, 1929.

Kürten stated: "Towards the end of September, 1929, at 8 o'clock in the evening, I waited for a victim on the Dreherstrasse, but not until about midnight did I see a woman approaching. I walked towards her, seized her throat and strangled her. We both fell down the bank into the field. I felt for the woman's sexual parts through her clothing. She shouted loudly for help. So I cleared out. I was chased. It was the only time I was ever pursued." Rad, who was born in 1901, said: "Kürten seized my sexual parts and wrenched them round, so that they were swollen. Otherwise his evidence was true." The hammer-blow cases Kürten described as follows:

CASE 63. THE MURDER OF IDA REUTER. 30.9.29.

"One Sunday I left home at 6 o'clock in the evening. I had pocketed a hammer. At the railway station I saw a young girl, accosted her and proposed a walk. We had a beer at Schumacher's and walked through the Hofgarten and over the Rhine bridge to the poplar wood. During this walk, night had fallen. Reuter hesitated to go any further. Therefore we turned back. Midway between the top of the wood and the playground, having made sure that nobody was around, I pulled the hammer from my hip pocket and hit the girl on the

right temple. For that purpose I had moved to the right side of
Reuter. Without a sound she collapsed. People were
approaching from the wood. I dragged Reuter from the dam
down to the meadows. Here I waited until the people had
passed. Meanwhile she had regained consciousness. She said:
'Let me alone.' Then I dragged her a good deal further. I gave
her other hammer-blows on the head, and misused her. I
pulled off her knickers to wash my hands with them in the
Rhine. I left Reuter and went back to the Hansaallee, taking
her little case with me. From it I took a ring for some future
girl acquaintance."
"After I got to the Rhine bridge I returned to the scene of the
crime, in order to drag Reuter down to the Rhine. I thought
she was dead. I seized her legs and dragged her towards the
river bank. But I noticed a man with a dog, so I cleared off
again."

CASE 64. THE MURDER OF DÖRRIER. 11.10.29.

"I left home on a week-day, about 9 o'clock in the evening,
putting the hammer in my hip pocket. By the Residenz theatre
I met a young, slim girl, who later told me her name was
Dörrier. I asked her to come for a walk. At first she did not
want to. In the end she went with me to Schumacher's. We
went by tram to Grafenberg and walked along the banks of the
Düssel. Dörrier was on my left. Suddenly I gave her a violent
blow on the right temple. In order to do so I stepped back.
Without a sound Dörrier collapsed. I grabbed her wrist and
dragged her several metres from the path. I then used her
sexually, after having pulled off her knickers from one leg. I
then gave her more heavy blows with a hammer on the head.
After the first blow she didn't say anything more, but only
groaned. I took off her cloak and also the hat which was very
bloody. I hid these things in the bushes." Later on these
articles were found. The sleeves had been torn out of the
cloak. With regard to this circumstance, Kürten made the
following comment: "You can see from that how excited I
was."

63

CASE 65. MEURER. 25.10.29.

"I left home at 8 o'clock in the evening. The hammer I used on Reuter and Dörrier I had hidden outside. I fetched it and pocketed it. In the Bruchstrasse I noticed a woman going down the dark Hellweg. I followed her and overtook her near the first new building. I started a conversation about the Egyptian darkness of the Hellweg and about the general unsafety. We arrived at the railway arch. As I knew these surroundings pretty well I had by that time made up my mind to commit the crime there. I stepped to the right side of Frau Meurer, took a step back and gave her a heavy blow with the hammer on the right temple. I don't know whether I actually hit the temple. The woman collapsed without a sound. I gave her more hammer blows as she lay on the ground. I took her attaché case and went back down the Hellweg. Later on I threw away the case."

CASE 66. FRAU WANDERS. 25.10.29.

"After the Meurer I did not go home but to the Hofgarten. I was accosted by a woman smoking a cigarette, who asked me to go with her. I went with her to the Ananasburg, where the path was concealed by bushes. Here Wanders stopped in order to have sexual intercourse with me. I turned her round, meanwhile taking the hammer from my hip pocket and struck her on the right temple. Without a sound Wanders collapsed and fell over the low railings. I then gave her several further blows on the head. In doing that the handle of the hammer broke and the head flew off into the bushes. I left Wanders lying where she was and went on. Wanders was repulsive to me, for I knew she was a professional prostitute and I never accost that kind of girl. After a quarter of an hour I returned to the place and searched in vain for the hammer."

"On the 27th of November, 1929, I set out with a pair of scissors about 5 o'clock at night. I met a little girl at the Ackerstrasse. I talked to her, and asked her quietly if she would come with me. We went into the open across some allotments as far as the wall of the Haniel's place. The child went with me quite willingly and did not cry. I seized the child's throat and strangled it. I stabbed it in the left temple. The child collapsed without a sound. With my left hand I held fast to her throat, knelt down and stabbed the child's breast with my scissors. With the right hand I felt the vagina, after having removed the knickers. Then I carried the body a few metres towards the Lenaustrasse and put it into the stinging nettles. I cleaned my hands on the wet grass. It was raining. There were no blood stains on me."
In February, 1930, the strangling crimes were resumed.

CASE 68. HILDEGARD EID. 23.2.30.

"I met a girl in the Schadowstrasse. We went to Schumacher's and then to Grafenberg. We spoke about sexual relations on a bench. She was very nervous. Suddenly at midnight I seized her by the throat and strangled her. She defended herself vigorously. I had sexual intercourse with her lying on the bench. I then accompanied her to her flat in the Cranach strasse. She promised she would not say anything about the strangling. On the following Sunday, the 2nd of March, I went again to the Cranach strasse to make sure that Hildegard had not reported the matter to any one. She was already leaning out of the window waiting for me. Together we visited several beer gardens. Then we went to my flat, undressed and went to bed. Before we had had sexual intercourse my wife returned unexpectedly. She remained quite quiet, merely asking the girl to dress herself, after which she took her back to the Cranach strasse." Eid was born in 1906. She confirmed all the points of this statement.

CASE 69. MARIANNE DAL SANTO

"In the middle of March, 1930, I offered to treat a girl to beer at Schumacher's. She told me she was not averse from perversions. We decided to practise some of these and for that purpose went to the Grafenberger Wald. There I suddenly strangled her. She defended herself: I could have anything I liked from her! I answered: 'I don't want anything from you' and strangled her again. But she managed to free herself and ran off."

S. commented as follows: "Kürten introduced himself to me as a well-to-do bachelor. He said I could sleep very nicely in his villa out of town. In the woods I wanted to turn back. He then suddenly seized me from behind by the neck and threw me to the ground and strangled me. I tried to appease him, but like lightning he seized me again. I fell to the ground. He stood over me with his legs spread. I kicked at him with my feet. I managed to release myself. I ran away and hid in the bushes. There I crouched from 10 o'clock till 6 in the morning. For hours I heard people passing the bushes, but I didn't see anybody."

CASE 70. IRMA BECKER.

"In March, 1930, I set out with the scissors. At the railway station a girl accosted me. I took her with me to Schumacher's and went with her to the Grafenberger Wald. She called herself 'Irma' and I reckon she was between twenty-two and twenty-four years old, and about 168 cm. high. Near the Hirschburg I seized her by the throat and throttled her violently. She defended herself vigorously and screamed. I pushed her down the bank to the Wolf ravine and cleared out."

Becker, who was born in 1907, deposed: "I arrived in Düsseldorf from Cologne and was accosted by a gentleman. We wanted to go to his flat. While in the woods I still believed that we were on the way to his flat. Kürten then said that he had only enticed me there and tried to pull me down on to a bench, pulled my dress up, tore my knickers down and seized my sexual parts. I defended myself and rearranged my clothes. He then wanted to lead me further on by the arm. After a few steps he pushed me forcibly down the slope. I called for help and rolled over and over several times until I reached the bottom. I had broken my umbrella beating Kürten when he tried to rape me."

CASE 71. SYBILLA WIL.

"On the 30th of March, 1930, I picked up a girl in the Königsallee. We chatted together on a bench in the Hofgarten; then we agreed to take a walk together on Sunday in the woods. During this walk we had sexual intercourse on a bench and I strangled her. As there were passers-by I cleared off." Wil, who was born in 1901, described Kürten as having behaved fairly decently. The sexual intercourse on the bench was scarcely completed because she was too frightened and pressed him back. She had not been throttled and Kürten had done no harm to her. He had accompanied her to Rath.

CASE 72. THE GIRL FROM HEME.

"At the station I accosted a graceful girl about twenty years old and 165 cm. in height. We went to a café and from there to Obercassel. In a deserted place I suddenly strangled her. She cried out loudly for help. I released her and made my way back to the station. When I alighted I saw that the girl was alighting, too. The following Sunday I saw her again in the Graf Adolf Strasse. I turned up Steinstrasse. Suddenly somebody seized me by the arm. 'You come along with me to a policeman!' I recognized the girl instantly and said: 'What about you coming with me to the policeman, too, to tell him about my purse which you stole with thirty marks in it?' With that I threw her off." This girl could not be traced.

"One Friday I became acquainted with a girl of thirty years of age in the Königsallee. I went with her into a cafe and then to the Hofgarten. We sat there until 11 o'clock. Suddenly I gripped her under her clothes. She smacked me in the face. I smacked her back." Hau returned home on a Saturday with a scratched nose and reported that she had been beaten and throttled by a man in the Hofgarten. In her examination on the 14th of June, 1930, she stated: "I became acquainted with a nice man, a builder's assistant, named Franz Becker. In the Hofgarten he made love to me. He drew me towards him and tried to feel under my skirt. With my clenched fist I punched his eye. He punched back with his fist, so that my mouth bled. He said: 'Is that what I get for treating you in the cafe?' I gave him three marks and he gave me back two marks fifteen pfennig. He kissed the blood from my mouth. He wanted to detain me longer, but I ran away. He shouted after me: 'Consider yourself lucky that we are not alone in the Hofgarten?'"

There followed three attempted attacks in which Kürten was disturbed. These were followed by the three final attacks.

CASE 77. CHARLOTTE ULRICH. 30.4.30.

"At 9 o'clock I picked up a girl in the street and went with her to Schumacher's and afterwards to the Grafenberger Wald. I lulled her suspicions by saying that there were always couples there. Where there is a broad view I gave her a blow with the hammer on the right temple. She collapsed, screaming loudly. I left her lying there. I saw this girl several times after that; the last time on the Wednesday before my arrest. The hammer I used was similar to the one I had used before. I struck with it several times and I saw the blood flow." I had occasion to examine Charlotte Ulrich in prison. She told me that on the 1st of May, towards midnight, Kürten accosted her on Graf Adolf Strasse and invited her to have a beer with him. In this way she missed the last train to Duisberg and was unable to

return home that night. As it was raining heavily, she accepted
his invitation; but she did not wish to go with him to his flat.
Kürten then proposed a nice night café. It was because she
was a stranger in the place that she became frightened in the
Grafenberger Wald, but Kürten reassured her: "Do you think,
maybe, that I am the Düsseldorf murderer?" he asked at a
point where the lights of the adjacent café were still visible.
So they went on until Kürten tried to throw her on to a bench,
when she defended herself. While the struggle was
proceeding, she saw how he unbuttoned his coat and thrust his
hand into his pocket. A little later she received a blow on the
side of the head, and she felt the blood pouring down her face
as from a tap. She then felt a second blow over the right
temple and then she lost consciousness. When she came to
herself again her hands were covered with blood and her bag
gone. She ripped up her petticoat and staunched the blood and
made her way towards the light and eventually reached the
railway station. There she asked a man for the first aid station,
but he advised her to go to the police. This she did not want to
do, for she was wanted by the police. In the end this man took
her to friends of his and these people cared for her for a
fortnight. Later, in fact, she spent three months in prison for
persistent stealing.
Ulrich also stated that her hands had been swollen and black,
and that the nail from the ring finger was missing. She had
raised her hand to her head to protect it from the hammer
blows. On both sides of her head Ulrich had fresh, pink scars,
angular in shape. Beneath them could be felt the fracture in
the cranium. It is amazing that this woman did not ask for
medical aid with such grievous wounds, and it is equally
remarkable that she was up and about again at the end of a
fortnight. This case provides a striking instance of the power
of the will to accelerate recovery.

"In the Schadowstrasse I became acquainted with a girl and we made an appointment for the following evening in the Rhine Park. We attempted to have sexual intercourse there on a bench, but there were too many people about. We therefore made an appointment for the following Sunday at Nordfriedhof. There a sudden thunderstorm came on, so Gertrud took me to her room. We had relations on her bed, but her mistress came knocking at the door, asking all kinds of questions. We then agreed on a meeting in her room for the 24th of May ... Meanwhile I was arrested."

Gertrud Bell: "Kürten called himself Franz Weidlich from the tramway depot. After we had sexual intercourse Weidlich was very nervous. I asked him to spend the night with me, but unsuccessfully. On the following Thursday I met him at the Worringerplatz. There he said that I was far too good for him, that, after all, I didn't know him at all, and that he was a bad man." Such is the notorious "great" confession which Kürten made after his arrest. Before the examining magistrate he varied it only in a few particulars. With me, too, he adhered to all his salient statements. As I have already remarked, the fullness of Kürten's confession awoke at first doubts as to his veracity. After he was lodged in prison and I had begun my observations of him, I referred in talk with him to these doubts. I propose to set forth these conversations here.

Kürten: "It is very easy to describe crimes one has not committed. Take, for example, the case of Gross, with which I had nothing to do at all. There I could have said, for instance, that on such and such a date I met a girl at the station I had to pass on my way home. She accosted me and took me with her to her room on Kurfürstenstrasse — and so on." Kürten next described the girl's room, the strangling and the actual circumstances.

Kürten: "I left the electric light burning. One could scarcely credit it that such a confession could be founded on the very full newspaper reports and yet be simply an invention. To that extent, I quite understand your doubts, Professor." I then asked Kürten why he had confessed fully in all the cases. He replied: "Professor, don't you understand that I am fond of my wife — that I am still fond of her? I have done her many wrongs; have been unfaithful over and over again. Yet, though my wife knew this quite well, she never let me down. My wife has never done any wrong. Even when she heard of the many sentences of imprisonment I have served, she said: 'I won't let you down, otherwise you will be lost altogether.' Professor, you know the big reward that was offered for my capture? At the police station we reckoned altogether twenty thousand marks, the arson rewards, together with the Government reward. It was then that I said to myself: If you confess only the case of the girl Schulte, which can be easily proved against you, you'll get at least fifteen years' imprisonment because of the bad prison record. I am forty-seven. After my release I would have been sixty-two. What could I make of my life at sixty-two? Life wouldn't mean anything at all, then. I had already finished with my life when I first knew the police were on my track. I wanted to fix up for my wife a carefree old age, for she is entitled to at least a part of the reward. That is why I entered a plea of guilty to all the crimes. But I could see that I might not be believed because of Stausberg."

Before the examining magistrate Kürten adopted another attitude with regard to his crimes. Whereas at the opening he adhered to his confession as set forth above, he made an unexpected change of front when confronted by his wife. On the 24th of June, 1930, he surprised the examining magistrate with the dramatic declaration: "I am not the Düsseldorf murderer." He had, he said, confessed to these crimes on the first occasion only to secure the reward for his wife. He then asserted that he had obtained all the details which he had given on his examination from the newspapers to which he had added his own free inventions. As Kürten was persistent, the examining magistrate had no choice, and had to make the best of a bad job and to put on the record all these cases which Kürten alleged he had concocted from newspaper reports.

71

Only one case, that of Hahn, did not fit into this fabric of lies, for no word of it had been published in the press. At last, thanks to the skill of the examining magistrate who succeeded in breaking him down, Kürten, after two months, reverted to his full confession.

Kürten: "Mr Examining Magistrate, you can take it as so, but believe me, that if I tell you the whole truth, you will hear a lot of horrible things from me." Kürten then amplified his confession in many ways, yet without revealing any new material of importance. His motive he kept as before: he wanted to revenge himself on society for the wrongs he had suffered in prison. In answer to the judge's question as to whether he had no conscience, Kürten replied: "I have none. Never have I felt any misgiving in my soul; never did I think to myself that what I did was bad, even though human society condemns it. As I have figured it out, when I am executed, my blood and the blood of my victims will be on the heads of my torturers, that is if there is such a thing as a Higher Justice. I have thought of the law of cause and effect, and on the law of the sufficient motive. There must be a Higher Being who gave in the first place the first vital spark to life. That Higher Being would also deem my actions good since I revenged injustice. The punishments I have suffered have destroyed all my feelings as a human being. That was why I had no pity for my victims."

But on another occasion, when alone with the examining magistrate, Kürten said: "I said before that I had no conscience. But I have got one. I felt it often. Even in these last years. It was when I committed adultery. Then I often thought how wrong it was of me with so hard-working a wife." I had Kürten under observation for the whole period of his imprisonment from June, 1930, until June, 1931. The most important of the discussions we had, I will set down in the following chapter. In this chapter the reader will hear Kürten speaking in his own words, in much the same way as he did in the confession set out in part above. I have changed his actual words very little, though here and there the subject matter has been assigned to the appropriate chapter.

CHAPTER III
FATE AND PERSONALITY OF KÜRTEN

On its surface the life of Kürten differs but little from that of a criminal psychopath. Born on the 26th of May, 1883, in Köln-Mülheim, he grew up in a bad environment. He was a good pupil in the primary school, learned the trade of his father, a moulder, and offended against the law for the first time at the age of sixteen. Four further sentences followed in quick succession. They were mostly for theft until 1904. During a short period of freedom Kürten confessed to four arsons in 1904. Then followed the long sentences of penal servitude — 1905 to 1913. This last sentence is only separated by a brief span of freedom in 1913 from the last sentence of seven years. Yet even this short interval is crowded by seven major crimes. In 1921, on being released from the penitentiary in Brieg, he went to his sister in Altenburg and settled down. There he found permanent work in a factory and married. There are four years of peace and decency. In 1925 his evil spirit lured him back to Düsseldorf and here he began his crimes with arsons and rapes which, in 1929, culminated in the monstrous offences.

I will now go into details:

(A) DESCENT.

The family history of Kürten was investigated by the examining magistrate. His father, now seventy-one, was a sand moulder and an efficient workman. But he was a drunkard and an uncontrolled, egotistic type. He always earned enough to keep his numerous children, though much of his money went on alcohol. The examining magistrate described him as a man who scarcely knew any moral restraints, yet demanded for himself every sort of respect, nor did he suffer contradiction or any challenge to his will. Even to-day, he impressed the examining magistrate by his self possession. His observations sometimes revealed humour and irony, coupled with an intense irascibility.

His manner of speech at his examination was abrupt and self-possessed. To sum up, he was formerly a heavy drinker, irascible and violent, and on that account several times in prison. Sexually uncontrolled, he had been imprisoned for incest with the eldest daughter, a sentence of eighteen months' penal servitude in 1897. Kürten's father had nine brothers and sisters, two of whom are supposed to have been drunkards. The grandfather was a railway worker. He was a hard-working man of peasant stock, but he drank and was a poacher. He was ultimately dismissed for theft and later sent to penal servitude.

The grandmother, on the paternal side, Elizabeth Kürten, died at seventy years of age; and she, too, was reputed to have been an alcoholic subject. Eight of the children of this couple reached ripe ages. Some of them had bad reputations for violence and drunkenness. The mother of Peter Kürten came of a respectable family. Her father was a hack proprietor. There were five brothers and sisters, all described as sane, physically and mentally, and who all lived to a ripe age. Mrs Kürten secured a separation from her husband following his attempted incest and imprisonment. In 1911 she married a joiner. She died in 1927.

The father of Kürten married for the second time in 1919 a working girl from whom he separated in the following year. Of the ten brothers and sisters of Kürten, two died young, one fell in the War. One of the sisters, Elizabeth, married young and became a good housewife. The other married sisters were described by Kürten as being very over-sexed. Two of the brothers served long prison sentences.

(B) KÜRTEN'S YOUTH AND PRISON SENTENCES.

Kürten: "In 1895 my parents moved to Düsseldorf Grafenberg and there I attended school. I passed easily and was a good scholar. Then I became an apprentice to a moulder. Father was a good workman, but also a hard drinker, hopelessly addicted to alcohol. It was customary in the foundry for people to drink hard, though it isn't so nowadays. The whole

family suffered through his drinking, for when he was in drink, my father was terrible. Windows were smashed, things were all broken up. I, being the eldest, had to suffer most. Often have I hidden away from his rage, either in the woods or in the school buildings. For weeks I would not return home. At those times I was a real vagabond. I used to steal money from women and Children out shopping. Once I was caught at it and should certainly have been sent to the reformatory but for the interference of my parents. As you may well imagine, we suffered terrible poverty, all because the wages went on drink. We all lived in one room. You will appreciate what effect that had on me sexually. Then poverty developed into bitter destitution when, in 1897, my father was sentenced to eighteen months' imprisonment for the crime of incest with his eldest daughter. When he came out of prison my father got his job back. I worked in the same foundry as an apprentice. There was never a Sunday for us, for on Sunday my father did all the odd jobs and I had to help him with them. He had installed a little foundry for making small aluminium articles in the cellar. Mother was good, decent, and respectable."
"When I look back and think of the married life of my parents to-day I really think that had they not been married one would have had to think of it as rape." "Father was not orthodox and wanted nothing to do with the Catholic religion. In short, my youth was a martyrdom. I was not even sixteen when I stole money from the factory and ran away. I never went back home after that. I don't want to omit describing my prison experiences because I am convinced that in the light of them my whole subsequent life can be explained. Once I had to do two days in prison. When I came out I was received by a police official who fettered me and led me through the whole town to the Berger Gateway. You can imagine what I felt like! I then came to know what it means to be without a roof to one's head."
"The crimes I began to commit then can be explained by sheer want. I stole to eat; got food under false pretences. In 1909 I got a week in prison, in 1910 six weeks, six months, three days, and so on, to the extent of three-quarters of the year.

75

Then came a long sentence — until 1914. It was then that I
became acquainted with disciplinary punishment in prison,
and of the severest kinds. It was terrible what I suffered under
it. I would describe it all as barbarous and I suppose most men
would do so to-day. Apart from the fact that hunger in
adolescence is real torture, I suppose there was some ground
for these sentences (for theft). I do not condemn those
sentences in themselves, but I do condemn the way they are
carried out on young people. The prison officials then were
quite different from those of to-day. Fettering was a common
form of punishment. Once I was fettered for three weeks. At
that time we had a lieutenant staying at the prison to be
educated as a prison inspector, and he had a lot of visitors to
whom he used to show the prison. I was taken out of the dark
cell and exhibited. The lieutenant made a little speech about
me, saying what a difficult prisoner I was. Once a clergyman
came. He fell on his knees and kissed my fetters."
"All that had a very bad effect on me, so that I can tell of
these things in full justification. Nothing is worse than the
spiritual suffering of one who is tortured through the infliction
of pain. For some of the things I did in prison I have no other
explanation than that I was not quite myself — a sort of
psychosis. Sometimes what I did was quite senseless. I had
cell madness. That resulted in my not being able to think
logically."
"I served all my sentences until 1903 in Düsseldorf. The
treatment of the prisoners was harder then than it is now. I
don't want to claim that all the punishments I got were all
inflicted unjustly. My anger and resentment were really
directed against the prison officials who got me into trouble
by their exaggerated reports on me."
"I dare say that frequently I did not do my work properly.
From 1905 to 1912, I spent much of my time spinning in my
cell in Münster prison. My rages in my cell, which occurred
periodically, were the result of harsh treatment. In Münster I
had a sort of prison psychosis. One day I rolled myself up in
silk under a table."

"In April, 1921, I was released from Brieg. Seven months of that sentence had been remitted because I carried a wounded official from the firing line on the occasion of a mutiny. On the other hand, I myself took part in another mutiny."

Very enlightening is the report of the head warder of the Brieg penitentiary. "Kürten," he said, "appreciated every situation at once, and when the favourable moment arrived, used it adroitly for his own advantage. He had no consideration for his fellow prisoners. He tried to hoodwink the prison officials by extreme sycophancy. For example, when the man who usually said prayers before the convicts fell ill, Kürten volunteered at once. It was astonishing with how much piety he recited the evening prayers. Once he threw a box of felt slippers at an overseer, 'You seem to think I am your messenger boy,' he said. He also tried to win the favour of the officials by betraying to them plans for attacks on them or of mutiny."

Here are the observations upon Kürten by the prison doctor: "On the 16th of January, 1907, Kürten lacerated the skin over the main artery with a knife and spoke a great deal of incoherent nonsense. This incident he pretends to have forgotten. In November, 1911, there is a note in his dossier describing a state of excitement observed by the physician in which Kürten spoke of suicide. I may add that Kürten's conduct in the prison was faultless in 1928."

Regarding this period a fellow prisoner says of Kürten: "Kürten was amiable and sly, he liked to hob-nob with the officials. He was also capable of being brutal. He talked a lot about his sexual adventures; he told how once he had bitten a woman's genitals until the blood came. He said, 'That's the greatest enjoyment one can get.' He then demonstrated how he would behave in doing it. He used to ask all the criminal sexual perverts questions and gave them advice, and told them how to conduct themselves on trial." Of this statement, Kürten asserts that it is pure invention. On the contrary, he said, he had always restrained himself and never given himself away to a fellow prisoner.

Nevertheless, we find this same prisoner coming to the police with his suspicions of Kürten after the murder of Hahn in November, 1929. Kürten was never so indiscreet in his talk again, though to another subsequent witness he dropped hints. This witness, Klauth, said: "Kürten thought a lot of his wife, but he also said, 'I like veal best, something I can really tease in the dark in quiet places.' I asked: 'Are you a pervert?' He answered 'Even old goats like to eat a green leaf now and then. A change is nice.'"

(C) MARRIAGE.

Kürten's wife was born in 1880 in Schlesien. She was the daughter of a tailor who was also a house owner. As a domestic servant she went to Berlin in 1896, got into bad company and was on that account brought home in 1897. There she earned her living as a factory worker.
In 1903 she began to have intimate relations with a gardener, a relationship which lasted for eight years. Although this man, to whom she became engaged, had promised to marry her, he jilted her in 1911. For this she shot him and was sentenced to five years' penal servitude.
Released in 1915, she remained in Leipzig until 1920, working as a dressmaker, and then took over a sweet shop in Altenburg. There she became acquainted with a sister of Kürten, and on the 12th of May, 1921, with Kürten himself. He was unsympathetic to her because he used to go about with other women. But as he threatened that he would push something between her ribs if she would not have sexual relations with him, she gave herself to him. As Kürten had a permanent job in 1923, they married. Frau Kürten also knew that her husband had involved himself with a certain girl named Oehler and that this girl threatened to bring a charge of rape against him. It was Frau Kürten who persuaded her not to take this course. Frau Kürten describes her husband as otherwise good. He had sent her money regularly from Düsseldorf. When she rejoined him after separation he confessed at once that he had been twice unfaithful, with the

girls Tiede and Mech. Yet despite her annoyance, he had gone off the following night with Tiede. Frau Kürten explained to Tiede that Kürten was a married man; but the Mech affair lasted until 1927, when Kürten was arrested. As to their conjugal life, Frau Kürten said: "Kürten was very excitable and then he bullied and shouted. But when I remained quiet, he, too, soon calmed down. For my part, I have taken all things as a punishment for my own old life. The Altenburg period was by far the best. There he was home-loving and took part in club life. It was in Altenburg that Kürten left the Catholic Church, but only because of the tax. Not until we came to Düsseldorf were we married in church. That was on the advice of the prison priest. But Kürten never wanted to hear about going to church or about God, either. In 1928 he wrote from prison that he had changed altogether, but when he was released he forgot all about that."

"Once, when I mentioned the murders and said that I was frightened, he wanted to see me home in the evening from the place where I worked. I never saw any trace of his crimes. He frequently had sexual intercourse with me, even against my will. In the last two years he was extremely keen on it. During this period he used to ask me to lie down naked."

In short, the marriage of Kürten had to withstand a good many strains. When the wife found her husband in bed with a strange girl, and when she saw him walking in the street with another girl, she forgave, so that one cannot help admiring the forbearance of this woman. But she knew well that with Kürten reproaches would be wasted. He would threaten suicide or lament that he had so little in life and yet that little was begrudged him by his wife. On the other hand, Kürten always spoke in a very nice way of his wife. He said to the examining magistrate: "My relations with my wife were always good. I did not love her in the sensual way, but because of my admiration for her fine character." This seems odd, for, on the whole, Kürten spoke badly about women. He went even so far as to hint that his own sister desired to have sexual relations with him; a conclusion he drew from her tenderness, her kisses and embraces.

CHAPTER IV
KÜRTEN THE SADIST

(A) THE MOTIVES OF KÜRTEN'S CRIMES AS REVEALED BY MEDICO-LEGAL EXAMINATION.

If one considers that, apart from the thefts which were dealt with by the courts, most of Kürten's crimes remained undiscovered, then one can understand that Kürten appeared to his acquaintances as a quite harmless being. Like every other worker in the factory, he did his work quietly, was seldom unemployed, was moderate and economical, did nothing to annoy his fellow workers. Yet, save for his wife, he had no human being who was dear to him, no friend, no comrade. His fellow-workers considered him vain. One witness described how Kürten always changed his clothes thoughtfully and carefully, standing before the mirror for a long time; how he used hair pomade and eau de cologne, and how sleek he then made himself look.

In fact, even in prison, Kürten always paid great attention to his appearance; he was slim and, comparatively, a good-looking man, with thick yellow hair always parted carefully, clever-looking blue eyes and, on the right cheek, a small scar the result of a quarrel in 1904, though this was not very noticeable. In 1922 Kürten sustained a head wound through a blow from a falling piece of iron. It left a scar of a finger-length on the skin of the scalp, and years afterwards Kürten complained of headache. Otherwise, there were no physical abnormalities.

As far as his psyche is considered, I always found Kürten of a pattern. That was already the case in 1928. As a prisoner awaiting trial he was generally amenable and quite frank with me — even confidential. Even when he was relating to me his experiences in the other prisons he remained calm, becoming only ironic. He was also always ready for the many enquiries and interrogations, and even after sittings which lasted hours, he showed no sign of fatigue or irritability.

To the police Kürten denied a sexual motive for his crimes.

He did not wish to be known as a lust murderer. So, too, before the examining magistrate, he made the admission that there was a sexual motive only towards the end of the enquiry, and then, in a very roundabout way. During my talks with him in prison, I soon succeeded in winning his confidence. I explained to him that so far as his trial was concerned what he revealed to the court was his own affair, but that what he revealed to me as the prison physician was protected as a professional secret. After turning matters over in his mind for some time, and not before he had asked of the examining magistrate the effect of Paragraph 300 of the Penal Code Manual, Kürten opened up to me in quite a different way about his motives. Of course, it was his intention that I should make use of these confidences, but only in such a way as to assist rather than damage his defence. But he gave me a completely free hand to make use of his statements for the purpose of science.

The ice having been broken, Kürten communicated to the psychologists his secrets — those secrets so carefully guarded at the time. They are of the utmost significance for an understanding of his psychological make-up.

In setting down Kürten's statements I merely directed his attention to its subject matter by interjected questions. I began with a question as to the motive for his crimes. In the beginning he denied to me, also, the sexual significance of these and invited me to believe his old motives, namely, vengeance on human society. But I explained to him that he was giving himself away starting each confession with the same formula "I went out to search for a victim," and so, too, with the termination — expiation for the wrongs done him. To that objection Kürten replied: "So far as the motives of my crimes are concerned, as I have so far described them, I took everything I said about my excitability and inner tension from books, namely, Lombroso. The statement of motive I made was the result of the trend of the Criminal Director's questions — he was so preoccupied with the psychological aspects of the case. Even so, I am bound to say that I did have a constant desire — you will call it the urge to kill — and the more the

81

better. Yes, if I had had the means I would have killed masses. I would have caused catastrophes. Every evening, when my wife was working late, I scoured the town for a victim. But it was not so easy to find one."

"The sexual urge was strongly developed in me, particularly in the last years and it was stimulated even more by the crimes themselves. For that reason I was always driven to find a new victim. Sometimes even when I seized my victim's throat, I had an orgasm; sometimes not, but then the orgasm came as I stabbed the victim. It was not my intention to get satisfaction by normal sexual intercourse, but by killing. When the victim struggled she merely stimulated my lust. For example, I would like to quote the case of Ohliger for which Stausberg was wrongly accused. I didn't have sexual intercourse with the child. It wasn't necessary because I had already ejaculated. The reaction had already set in while I was throttling Ohliger, but not ejaculation. It was only while I was stabbing her that the excitement ended in ejaculation. I had my member out and ejaculated without erection, which is much nicer; that happened, too, with Hahn, and gave me a shudder down the whole back. I want to explain to you also, Professor, about your conclusions as to the sexual parts of the child Ohliger. When I was throttling the child, I inserted my middle finger into the vagina. I had pulled down the little knickers a bit and later on rearranged them. But I did not feel anything — only when I took the scissors and stabbed I had an ejaculation. In handling the child I might have introduced some seminal fluid with my finger — which you found later on — that was the first case. At midnight I went back to the body. I wanted to touch it. I won't deny that I did it to get fresh sexual excitement, but there was no more ejaculation. Another thing, I only fingered her over her clothing. I could not stay long because my wife was bound to come home." I now directed Kürten's attention to the burning. "That, of course, I did not do to destroy the body by fire. I got sexual excitement in doing it but no ejaculation. The following morning at 9 o'clock I returned once more, when she had been found. I then saw the officials and the crowd of people and I nearly had an ejaculation, but not quite. That I wasn't out for normal sexual enjoyment you can tell from the Scheer case. That was a man."

"I was scouring the Hellweg for a victim. I saw a man coming along. I thought 'That's a suitable Subject.' Not a soul to be seen anywhere! The man was staggering. He bumped into me. He was drunk. I stabbed him with the scissors. At the first stab in the temple he fell down. Then at once I got sexual excitement, and the more I stabbed the more intense it became. I gave him a severe stab in the neck and I heard distinctly the faint gushing of his blood. That was the climax. Then came the ejaculation. I stopped stabbing and just rolled the body over the bank."

"The following morning, when I went back, the Murder Commission was there. Then I enjoyed another ejaculation despite the intense cold. As you know, it was horribly cold at that time. Yet I was not conscious of it, though I had on only a very thin coat. When I am in that condition I am not even conscious of fatigue. During my long night prowlings, when I covered long distances, I was so intent upon my purpose that I never noticed any fatigue at all. And that despite the fact that I had been at work throughout the day."

"You have asked me when I first detected in myself a tendency to cruelty. Well, that goes back decades. When I was a child I did not torture animals, at least, not more than other boys do. Of course, we went birds-nesting and caught frogs. But I was prematurely developed sexually and at the age of fifteen or sixteen I was already like that, then I used to stab sheep, for instance, that were grazing on the Grafenberger meadows. When I did that I realized that it gave me an agreeable feeling, but without any ejaculation. That was the start of it all, and the first time that I became conscious of the connection between cruelty and the sexual urge. I had also at that time cut off the head of a dog. Then I realized that there was something nice in it. You can imagine that, Professor, and you must try it for yourself sometime — how the blood rushes absolutely silently when you cut off the head of a goose. The origin of this feeling goes back a long way. When we lived in

Köln-Mülheim a dog catcher lived in the same house. At that time there was one in every town. The dogs were captured, slaughtered and eaten. The lard was sold as a specific, being used to fix cobwebs over wounds. This dog-catcher used to torture the dogs he caught. For instance, he used to prick them with a needle or break off their tails, saying that he wanted to see whether the animals were healthy. I watched this frequently and enjoyed it. I was then nine years old. This dog-catcher also showed me how you make the dogs attached to you, taught me how to play with the dog's genitals until it ejaculated. An animal like that can't be beaten away. Later, when I was thirteen, I often thought about that dog-catcher while I was taking young buzzards and owls from their nests with other boys, or when I caught squirrels or martens. Those we sold to the dealer Otten on the market — I suppose you know it. And we made a nice bit of pocket money in that way. I still have a scar on my finger where a squirrel once fastened his teeth on me. I had to compress his neck to make him let go. In handling it like that I had an ejaculation, although only a boy of fourteen. Later, by reading and through talk, I learned about this sort of thing. Seeing blood gave me a pleasant feeling. At that time the slaughter of pigs in people's homes was more frequent than it is now, and I always liked to watch it. Already, as a schoolboy, I loved to see fires. The shouting and the excitement were fun to me. Whether my youthful onanism had anything to do with it, I don't know. That was not very important, it was only temporary. By the time I was thirteen I knew all about sexual matters, and in my own home I saw my parents have sexual relations. Of course, I soon decided that I would try for myself. I began first with a schoolgirl and got as far as contact with the naked body, but not to proper intercourse, as the girl resisted and moved about too much. In this way it occurred to me to try it with animals. There were goats in the stables and also a good many sheep used to be kept penned. For this purpose I went to neighbouring stables where it was easy for me to get in. I actually did have intercourse with female animals; I did actually force my member into the animal. Then later I thought no more of it. It was only a temporary thing about the age of thirteen."

"Soon after that I became aware of the pleasure of the sight of blood. Today it is not clear to me why I went to the stables beyond the Hirschburg. The house is still standing there. I stabbed a pig in the back, it bled terribly and squealed. Then I was seen and recognized because the son of the house and I were school fellows. There was a terrible row about it at home."

"It was in my thirteenth year that for the first time I secured a complete orgasm by wounding. I attempted sexual intercourse with a sheep; whether it succeeded or the sheep would not keep still, I forget. I stabbed the sheep and at that moment ejaculated. I repeated that frequently for two or three years. After that I only had connection with females. That was at Coblenz."

"It was after that that I ran away with embezzled money and was accosted on the street by a girl of about eighteen years of age. We lived together until the embezzled money was all gone. The sexual intercourse we had then was quite normal. Yet, even then, I pinched the girl, for wounding was not yet the essential condition for success in the intercourse. In Coblenz at that time I was not very strongly drawn towards the girl; in three or four weeks we had relations only a few times. That seems rather strange for a young man."

"Then came the first imprisonment. Even at that time I had thoughts about wounding, but they were not insistent. When I came out of prison I became acquainted by chance with a woman and her daughter of sixteen. It was the woman who attracted me, but I paid no attentions to the daughter. That seems rather strange. The intercourse with the woman succeeded only when I ill-treated her. In the beginning she put up with it, but when it became worse and I threatened to kill her, she gave me away to the police and I was punished for using threats and failing to keep the domestic peace. I got one week."

"During my first long sentence for theft, one of eight months, I was separated from this woman. Then I met her again in

1904 and started up with the daughter. I ill-treated her and threatened her with a revolver. It was an out-of-date old thing that would not have been capable of hurting her. I had great fun as they ran away and I sent shots after them. While I was doing that I ejaculated."

"Another shooting occurred at that time. While I was in prison I had figured out how I would shoot a girl I knew in Grafenberg. At that mere thought I felt sexual excitement. I had known this girl at school. I studied the place where she lived and actually waited for days in order to kill her. One morning I watched her from their courtyard how she got out of bed and then I shot at her. After a while, when things quietened down again, I fired again that evening through the window. Then I fled to the Grafenberger Wald, was chased and arrested and found with the weapon. I confessed and got a year's imprisonment."

I directed Kürten's attention to the throttling cases:

"I told you already that throttling in itself was a pleasure to me, even without any intention to kill. Take, for example, the Schäfer case in 1913 (compare Case 7). I had taken this girl out frequently and at last we spent the whole night in the Grafenberger Wald. I then throttled her several times and she did not mind. I just calmed her down: 'This is all part of love,' I said, 'I don't want to kill you.' It was only the beginning, when I inserted my member in her vagina on the bench; it was in the wood that I had an ejaculation, and then without sexual connection at all."

"It was just the same in the case of Franken in 1913. (Case 11.) There, too, I throttled the girl for some time and saw how the blood spouted from her mouth and in that way got my ejaculation. In other cases I did not achieve my end by throttling; for instance, Maas, (Case 50) I throttled her violently, too, but she freed herself and ran away."

When I asked Kürten whether he had ever throttled any of his victims to death, he replied that he thought he had done so in the case of the Ohliger child because she did not move after the throttling. He said, also, that in August, 1929 (Case 53), he had throttled Annie for so long that he thought she was dead

and he had then thrown the body into the Rhine in order to
conceal traces of his crime.

Kürten then spoke of the effect of imprisonment upon him:
"The long sentences I served when still quite young had a
very bad effect on me. Other prisoners think of naked women
and masturbate. This I did very seldom. I got no pleasure from
it. I got my climax of enjoyment when I imagined something
horrible in my cell in the evenings. For instance, slitting up
somebody's stomach, and how the public would be horrified.
The thought of wounding was my peculiar lust and it was in
that way that I got my ejaculations. I can remember exactly
how it happened in 1905 in the prison at Metz. There, for the
first time, I got an ejaculation by thinking of grievous
woundings and the actual killing of people. That went on for
years. If I hadn't had that I would have hanged myself. There
is really nothing astonishing about the fact that, having got out
of prison, well used to such imaginings, I was urged to do the
things. You remind me, Professor, of the Mülheim crime. It is
certain that just then I had seven years in Münster behind me.
Actually, I had gone out to steal and the murder was
incidental. But you are quite wrong, Professor, if you think
that this crime stands as a single case in those years. No, one
thing and another happened, but there were no big jobs. But
when the decision came, it came suddenly because of the
opportunity — in contrast to the last years when the urge has
dominated me continuously. The child Klein (Case 7) lay in
her bed asleep. I seized her throat, and at once my sexual
excitement began. During the throttling I grasped the child's
vagina with my fingers in order to tear it open, but it was not
enough for my lust: I cut the throat. It is the blood that is
decisive in most of the cases, throttling alone is insufficient to
produce ejaculation. There is, for instance, the case of the
Italian. I only know her Christian name, Marianne. She could
satisfy herself by sucking, but I got no pleasure out of that, so
I throttled her for about ten minutes, but without success, for
she did not scream, but defended herself vigorously. (Case
69.) Then, again, the case of Anna Ist, I treated her so badly

that she was black and blue. Yet even after that she went out with me again. Some women are funny!"

"I can't say, Professor, that there were periods when my urge was stronger or weaker. Only during the period of hunger in Brieg prison I became a walking corpse and had no desire for sex. That is why nothing had happened at Altenburg. I only ill-treated women in order to get an ejaculation, but without complete sexual intercourse. It was only when I came to Düsseldorf and began to have relations with Tiede that I indulged more frequently in cruelty. In the beginning Tiede put up with it. Then, when she learned that I was married, she charged me with it. Besides her I had Mech and Kiefer in the Parkstrasse at the same time. When there seem to be long gaps in the list of my crimes I confess it is due to the terms of imprisonment, or to the fact that I failed in some projected assault. There are smaller attempts in between which I do not remember clearly myself and therefore have either not confessed or divulged. It was during this period that I committed arson on many occasions. I did not reveal all of the arsons during the investigation by the police. I then gave another reason for these crimes, but that was because it was more or less suggested to me and out of egotism I did not contradict them. It is not true that I wanted to kill the vagabonds sleeping in the haystacks I fired. It is the fact that I had no such thought. In my imagination arson played the same role as other mass accidents; when the people dashed about screaming I enjoyed it immensely. The bright glow of the fire at night was exciting, but one thing is certain, the frequency of the cases in these last years was due to the injustice of the sentences I served. When in 1926 I was sent to the remand prison I was absolutely mad. I had the feeling that I was innocent. To that feeling there were added imaginings of a sexual kind. Therefore, after my release in 1927 many more arsons took place than are mentioned on the list here. Besides, in addition to the case of Ist, there were minor cases of attempted throttling. In 1927 I was sentenced again for false pretences, which wasn't false pretenses at all. Tiede had sworn falsely. In 1928 I again suffered an unjust prison sentence for alleged threats and insults. I was absolutely innocent. I resent that even to this day. You will now realize, Professor, why there were frequent arsons from 1927 onwards."

"I must answer your question whether I was suspected by any one with a 'No.' I revealed everything after my arrest and without being asked. I don't want to pretend to you, Professor, that a desire to boast had not something to do with that confession — it was a bit of Kürten senior coming out in me. You must try to put yourself in my place. The highest police officers were hemming me in. They all marvelled at me as a miracle. That is why I took on me more than was really true."

"For instance, the murders in Altenburg, the details of which are fresh in my memory from gossip. They often marvelled at my memory. Things that happened twenty or thirty years ago I can describe to you with every detail. I can recall the day and the hour of every arson I committed. But the statements which I made previously about wanting to kill the down-and-outs sleeping in the haystacks by firing them are true only in so far as I had no original intention of killing people in that way. During the firing itself the thought that human beings might be burnt added to the sensations that I experienced. I always watched the fires, usually from near at hand, so near in fact that I have been asked to give a helping hand. Otherwise I was among the spectators of the street ... The shouting of the people and the glare of the fire pleased me. During big fires I always came to an ejaculation. If you see in the list sometimes several arsons in one evening, then I had had no success with the first or the second. I also ejaculated when I fired the woods. It was a lovely sight when one pine after another was consumed in the flames fanned by the sharp East wind ... that was wonderful."

"At the arson in the Wolfsaap I had no success in the beginning, so I left it and made my way to the Stützhof farm and set a barn alight. But as the barn was some distance and isolated, there were few people about, for the people were all at the Wolfsaap. So I went back again to the barn. Meanwhile some excitement had started up. Fire engines came up, rumbling; the tiles of the roof cracked with the heat and the reports of them bursting resounded to the borders of the woods. The owls then hooted and I ejaculated. Again, when I fired the peat belonging to the Heumieten (Case 29), there was not enough noise. A policeman had to come and arouse the people and even then they didn't get up. That is why that same evening I set fire to the Hohenzollern colony. That was another matter altogether. The whole colony crowded together and I ejaculated. I tried to set fire to the Düsseldorf Orphanage several times, but the fire always petered out again. I probably ought not to have done it because of the orphans."

"The three arsons of January 1929 that took place on the same evening (Cases 42-44) also came about because it was too quiet at the first fire at the Papendell haystack. The second fire at the barn in the field did not catch and only at the third fire, when the stack was blazing and there was a great commotion, did I have success."

I led the talk once more back to his sexual acts:

"You ask me how it is possible for me to have normal sexual intercourse at all. Well, if I don't ill-treat the woman during the intercourse, then I get no orgasm. Even with my wife I had to use a sort of fantasy, otherwise I was impotent. It was usually my wife who took the initiative for intercourse. After we had been married six months she used to say: 'Are we married or aren't we?' She has always had to help me to get an erection and even then, in order to succeed, I had to conjure up all kinds of fantasies and then it took a long time. So, too, with my victims, I never succeeded without brutalities, not even with Hahn. She believed that I had had complete intercourse with her, but I did not ejaculate. Without violence my member slackens quickly in the vagina. It was so with Butlies and the others with whom I was supposed to have had complete connection."

I next spoke to Kürten about the single cases that took place, one after the other, for so far he had not mentioned them. The statement he made was as follows:

"I have told you already that the main thing with me was to see blood. Here I must tell you of another recent case.

Whenever I happened to be near a serious accident in the street I felt sexually excited. A short time before I was arrested I saw a brakesman fall from the freight wagon of a street car on Erkrather Strasse, and go under its wheels. The blood gushed out and I pretended to assist the victim. I then had an orgasm. Such cases happen frequently, even with animals. Thus, once on the corner of the Mintropstrasse I saw a horse that had been knocked over by a tram. The animal bled to death. By chance I saw it all and ejaculated."

"Whether I took a knife or a pair of scissors or a hammer in order to see blood was a matter of indifference to me or mere chance. Often after the hammer blows the bleeding victims moved and struggled, just as they did when they were throttled. I never got an orgasm at the start of these proceedings and for that reason I had to continue them. For instance, the Albermann case (Case 67), I felt nothing while actually throttling. That was why I repeated what I did in the Mülheim case, putting my fingers into the child's vagina. On that erection took place at once, and I then introduced my member into the vagina of the child. That was only an attempt, for my member relaxed again and I had to stab. Then only ejaculation took place. I can hear the bleeding, even when the stabbing is through the clothing, into the heart."

"It was thus as I lay on the Albermann child, my member still in the child's vagina, while I continued to stab her breast. It was similar, too with Hahn. There, too, I had no satisfaction during the sexual act, only later on during the throttling I became stiff again and when, as I stabbed her throat, the blood gushed from the wound, I drank the blood from the wound and ejaculated. I probably drank too much blood because I vomited. The Hahn girl was still alive, despite the terrible loss of blood. Finally, to kill her, I stabbed her in the breast and again I heard the gushing of blood. My return twice to this girl's body was for purposes of security: the body could not be left in the stream. As I carried the body to the grave which I had dug I thought about crucifying her. I had taken strong staples with me and wanted to nail the body to a tree with outspread arms. But I had not time. That, of course, was warranted to stir up some excitement. I then stood in her grave and drew the body down to me. In fingering it and holding it firmly — the under part was naked — I became once more sexually excited and had an orgasm. It struck me that the body was not stiff, but quite flaccid. She hung limp over my shoulder when I carried her. What cause prevented *rigor mortis* from developing?"

"I must now answer your question whether simple stabbing was sufficient to satisfy my sexual desire, and I must answer 'yes.' For example, when I was going after Anna Goldhausen I got sexual excitement on turning the corner and going towards her as she came towards me. I had an erection as I stabbed her, but no orgasm; therefore I went on stabbing. I had no satisfaction when I stabbed Frau Mantel because the woman shouted so terribly that I had to run away as fast as I could. Only in the third case of stabbing did I have an orgasm — that of Kornblum — but without complete erection. Afterwards my wife discovered the spots on my clothes in the same way as she discovered it in the case of Hahn and reproached me with it."

"Also with Frau Kuhn I had an orgasm despite the fact that it was bitterly cold and that the whole attack took but seconds. With the Flehe children the throttling and struggling of the little Hamacher had an exciting effect and the sound of the blood when I cut her throat made me ejaculate. With the older child, Lenzen, it was the resistance that excited me and finally the stabbing which brought the climax, but without erection."

"That evening I was already in a state of strong sexual excitement. Again, the day after the crime, when I visited Flehe and saw the tremendous excitement of the people, I ejaculated."

(All this Kürten told me in the summer of 1930.
When, in February, 1931, I referred again to the murder of the children, Kürten was doubtful if he had ejaculated twice within such a short period as he has stated above. But I am of the opinion that his first account is correct as the sound of the gushing blood had been always an infallible means with him.)

"The Schulte case (Case 59) on the following day, did not differ from the others. My sexual lust was appeased because of what had happened the day before, and it was only in the dark, during the shouting, cutting and stabbing that I had an orgasm."

"In the case of Reuter, too, I ejaculated. (Case 63.) The girl had collapsed after the first hammer blow and then when I had dragged her away from the path she regained consciousness and bit and struggled. It was through that that I became excited even without the shedding of blood. Even so, I had to continue striking with the hammer, for I had had no ejaculation when I had connection with her. It was much the same with Dörrier when she was lying unconscious after the first hammer blow. I had already exposed myself, had an erection, and had already penetrated her, but even then I had to keep on striking with the hammer until I ejaculated. I also gripped her neck with my left hand."

Here, too, I want to mention that Kürten gave a totally different account of the Dörrier affair in February, 1931. He then denied the coitus altogether and said that he did not even penetrate and that he had only attempted to do so. He said that in uncovering her he had seen her bloodstained linen and concluded that she was at her period and therefore checked himself from any further advance. This alternative account is noteworthy, since it does not explain the vaginal injury of Dörrier.

"In Wanders' case (Case 66), the excitement had no climax because the hammer broke — her head was harder than the hammer." (During one of the last interviews I had with Kürten prior to the jury trial, he himself referred to the blood-drinking.)

"I have already told you, Professor, of the Hahn case and how I drank the blood from the wound of her neck. As I told you, I stabbed her throat and, lying across her, I drank the blood that gushed out. While I did that I thrust my scissors with my right hand several times into her breast." (That explains the oblique direction of the stabs I found on the body.)

"In the case of Ohliger I also sucked blood from the wound on her temple, and from Scheer from the stab in the neck. From the girl Schulte I only licked the blood from her hands. It was the same with the swan in the Hofgarten. I used to stroll at night through the Hofgarten very often, and in the spring of 1930, I noticed a swan sleeping at the edge of the lake. I cut its throat. The blood spurted up and I drank from the stump and ejaculated."

"Your question too, Professor, whether the recollection of my deeds makes me feel ashamed, I will tell you."

"Thinking back to all the details is not at all unpleasant. I rather enjoy it. To be sure, I pity the victims, but in conjuring up the memories in my imagination I even succeed in getting sexual satisfaction. These explanations, Professor, are only intended for you as a scientist, for I have told you with complete frankness my innermost feelings. Such things are not good for the public. They can do only harm and certainly no good. It was on this account that at my trial I put forward other explanations of my crimes. That may at least do some good towards the reform of the penal system."

"So far as my own fate is concerned I am tranquil. It is because of that that I am able thus quietly to answer your question whether I am not sorry for my confession with 'No.' It is better that I made an end of it. I would not have stopped my attacks. I was impelled over and over again. But I also want to point out that I was able to master my urge. Therein lies my guilt — that I did not do it in the murder cases. I know quite well that there I am guilty. Therefore I want to shoulder my punishment. After having spent twenty four years in such institutions I prefer death to pardon. Though prison is different to-day from what it was in earlier times I see the contempt on the faces of the prison officials and the other prisoners. Those men, Professor, don't understand, as usual. But, after all, people are right when they say: 'The beast! The wild animal!'"

It was on this occasion that Kürten asked me particularly about the execution in detail — whether, his head chopped off, he would still hear the gushing of blood. That would be for him, he said, the pleasure of all pleasures.

It was while he was awaiting trial that Kürten changed this attitude towards death. The frequent interviews with physicians and lawyers probably had something to do with this change. Shortly after the jury-trial I once more asked of him what verdict he anticipated; and whether he would prefer a life sentence to death. He answered: "That depends, Professor, on whether the court finds for murder or manslaughter. From the legal standpoint murder presupposes deliberation. This I certainly deny in the Mülheim case; that was a spontaneous act done quite blindly. Such a deed is no premeditated murder."

"As to the later cases I shan't have any such luck with that plea. It will be difficult for them to consider those cases as manslaughter. It is difficult, Professor, to answer your question about the death sentence. When a man has been sobered up after the event, as I have been, he lets thing go their own way. If the Ministry confirm the death sentence, well, then I shall be executed; but if there is the slightest ground for the view of legal irresponsibility, then there might be some chance for a petition for pardon."

"After all, an execution does not achieve much. It is doubtful whether they can wash off with my blood the blood I have shed. It boils down in the end to an act of vengeance which the people have asked for. When I myself think about my deeds, and in particular about the children, then I abhor myself so much that I am impatient for my execution. That's the way you feel when you sober up. On the other hand, capital punishment itself is criticized even by the legal experts, so that one says to oneself: 'What, chop off a man's head simply because the people shout for it?'"

Now there is revealed to us a Kürten utterly different from the man interrogated by police and judge. These crimes, hitherto incomprehensible, become comprehensible, the wrong-doings of an abnormally directed sexual urge. The criminal becomes the sadist, but nothing fundamentally new for sexual pathology is opened up by Kürten's crimes. Qualitatively, he does not differ from other sadistic criminals; only quantitatively, but quantitatively he stands out as a man unique in recent criminal history. Indeed, to an extent that justifies a more detailed examination of the man's sadism.

(B) ANALYSIS OF KÜRTEN'S SADISM AND OF HIS MOTIVATION.

Of the sexual perversions sadism alone is of outstanding importance in forensic medicine, for with sadism sexual intercourse itself is either complicated with acts of violence or acts of violence lead to the stimulation of sexual lust in place of the normal sexual act. The medico-legal expert encounters sadism in many degrees from the acts which accompany coitus itself, such as a wild gripping and pressing with the fingers into the flesh of the woman, to the biting and violation, the killing and dismemberment. It is common to all sadists that they cannot achieve orgasm without violence. They differ merely in the types of these acts of violence, most of them adhering to a single method which they use repeatedly. In this category come the hair-cutters, the clothes-destroyers, the knife-stabbers. Among the most dangerous sadists are the actual lust murderers and these, one finds, usually proceed according to a prescribed method. This was, at all events, the case with those lust murderers whom I had under observation. I need only recall the case of Tripp, well known through the press. The characteristic of the professional criminal sadist enunciated by Heindl is true also of the sadistic criminal. He commits his deeds always by the same method. Nothing avails to deflect the professional criminal from his habitual *modus operandi*, even when he knows that to follow it involves his ruin. Again and again, as though under compulsion, he reverts to his specific method.
Heindl's judgement is right in principle and applies to Kürten's case, with this proviso: Kürten differed from the average sadist in that he pursued *different methods of violence* alternatively.

But this seems an exception from the rule. The changes in method of procedure in Kürten's case spring from his general criminal nature and are the result of his preoccupation with protecting himself against discovery. He has said himself that in this way he would be able to create the impression that several men had been active in the Düsseldorf crimes. Furthermore, his change of weapon was the natural consequence of the breaking of his dagger and his hammer, neither of which could be replaced without grave risk of discovery. He was even at pains to hide his daggers and hammers in the open and to take back to his lodgings only the innocuous household scissors.

Kürten's sadistic tendencies are revealed quite early in his childhood in his love and enjoyment of the spectacle of animal slaughter. For he claims to have first experienced lust under such circumstances. Thus his next step was determined, namely, to attack an animal himself. In this period, the thirteenth to the fourteenth years of his life — comes the episode of bestiality which lasted, however, so short a time that he was unable to say which sexual stimulus was the first. It seems certain that he soon abandoned his attempts at coitus with sheep and goats in favour of sexual stimulation by means of the sight of blood. He himself says that already at the onset of puberty he was familiar with the process of augmenting his lust by stabbing the animals with which he committed bestiality, but that in course of time he had abandoned bestiality altogether. The sight of the gushing blood, and the hearing of the noise made by it, remained his peak point of enjoyment to the last. As Kürten reports, shortly and very vividly, in Case 13: "The drunk man sat on the bench. I approached him from behind and struck him with the sharp edge of the axe. He fell over. I took cover and saw how he bled. I then ejaculated."

Note well that it was not the ruthless blow with the axe, but the sight of the blood that produced the effect. That was the infallible means of exaltation with him, even when other often-tried means, such as throttling, hammer blows, etc., failed to produce any effect, or did not produce an effect quickly enough. Thus with the sixteen-year-old Franken he says: "I throttled her several times. I saw blood come from her mouth and I then had an orgasm." So, too, in the cases of Ohliger, Albermann, and Hahn. This was the stimulating factor that produced the second surge of lust almost before the first had exhausted itself — Hamacher and Lenzen — and was so quick, indeed, that he did not even have an erection. Kürten does not wish to be regarded as a child or animal torturer in the ordinary sense of the word. The cruelty to animals, as he describes it, was, however, already sadistically directed. Very soon he used violence against the big animals as well. Thus he confirms established experience that the early tormenting of animals is a sure sign of future criminality. Just as monstrous as his torturing of animals in youth had been, so his crimes were to become at a later period. Very soon Kürten became familiar also with the lust producing effect of the glare of fire, a fact which explains his frequent arsons. But this effect was not conditioned only by the flames, at least not later on in his life when in order to achieve the highest climax of lust he had to have in addition the spectacle of the anguish of the victim of his crime.

This brings us to the second component of Kürten's sadism: the cruelty. We know that sexual lust and cruelty are neighbours in the Empire of Feeling. The infliction of some degree of pain during coitus is frequent with the man. But it is not the essential prerequisite for the success of the sexual act: it remains ancillary.

It is very different with the sadist Kürten, for with him the more violent the struggle with the victim the more certain his success. He frequently ascribes the ejaculation to the struggles and resistance of the children. To the investigating magistrate Kürten said: "When I strangled my victim first it was because of my tender heart. I did not want it to appear that I had tortured my victim."

This self-praise can be regarded merely as an attempt to buttress up his suggested motive of revenge. He did not advance such excuses to me or to the other physicians.

According to his confession to the police, Kürten must have appeared as a murderer whose objective it was deliberately to destroy his victims. And the motive of vengeance he advanced, and his alleged desire to excite horror in the public mind, fitted the facts, apparently. But as an expression of sadism these crimes underwent a complete change of character. They were committed solely in order to satisfy his sexual urge. The orgasm being achieved, the interest of Kürten in his victim was usually extinguished. Where he occupied himself further with them it was either to cover up traces of his crime or to search for new lust stimuli, after an interval. In illustration of the first case I may cite that of Heer (Case 60). At the hearing before the police Kürten said: "I throttled Lina — she freed herself and I throttled her again, and again did not succeed. I then pushed her into the Düssel." From these words, of course, the logical inference is that it was a plain lust murder. But to me Kürten said that the second throttling had been crowned with success, that is, he achieved an orgasm and thereafter had but one objective — to be rid of Heer. ("The bitch" was how he once referred to her.) It must have been quite clear to so crafty a criminal that she would not be drowned in the shallow Düsselbach.
(As examples of the recurrent lust excitement note the cases of Ohliger, Hahn, and the return of Kürten to the graves of his victims.)
All the various cruelties which Kürten practised served only the single purpose of achieving an orgasm. Let us examine the series of crimes in this light. The throttling cases are straightforward. He throttles the girls until ejaculation, he then releases them. In order to mask his perversion from the woman, and to conceal the real significance of the proceedings, he sometimes feigned coitus. But it is only *intromissio sine ejaculatione* as in Case 7. The girl Schäfer, of course, had her own interpretation of the throttling attempts. She says: "In order to make me submissive he throttled me." But Kürten explained the affair differently:

"What happened on the bench was only the beginning. I was in her, but I did not achieve my aim. Only after repeated throttling did I do so."

Thus, too, in Case 17, the coitus with Kiefer in the laundry was but a preparatory action. Here, too, his confession is as follows: "I throttled her during intercourse with the intention of killing her. I did not succeed."

Kürten expressly drew my attention to the fact that the addition made in his confession to the police — "I had a revolver with me" — was a lie. He said: "I did not even possess one. I only said that out of bravado."

In several cases of throttling, Kürten found that things did not turn out as he had reckoned. For instance, in Case 17 Wack, Case 22 Ist, Case 50 Maas, and Case 72 (the girl from Heme), as these young women were able to free themselves from his throttling grip and to cry out. In other cases Kürten claims that he achieved his purpose by throttling alone. Thus, in Case 52, in the Freitagstrasse: "I throttled her a long time until I came, then I released her because there were people about."

In Case 62 (Rad) Kürten had throttled the victim and bruised the vulva: "The orgasm took place without erection." Here the stout defence of the woman and the rough treatment of the vulva and the infliction of pain achieved the end. Here, too, the tragi-comic meeting with Hau comes in. (Case 73.) When Kürten, seated on the bench in the Hofgarten, felt under the girl's skirts, she slapped his face. He retaliated and made her bleed. He then kissed the blood from her mouth and ejaculated. Kürten keeps silent as to the comic end of the scene, in which he made the girl pay for the coffee which he had bought her.

In Case 68 (Eid), the girl apparently submitted to the throttling attempts because, despite them, she was drawn to Kürten. Kürten himself says that during the coitus on the bench he had an orgasm — "because I throttled her during the act."

In Case 69, it was again the violent defence put up by Santo which brought Kürten to the sexual climax. It was much the same in Case 70 (Becker). During the struggle in the wood, when the attacked girl smashed her umbrella over Kürten's head, Kürten achieved satisfaction, and having achieved his climax he cared no more for Becker, pushed her away from him and down the slope, just as he had dealt with Heer previously.

Actually, these abrupt dismissals of the girls were far from being part of Kürten's sadistic programme — that was completed with the orgasm. If, after that, the throttled girls remained comparatively friendly, Kürten, too, became the polite gentleman he was before.

The last rape, that of Butlies, is the best illustration of this. When he throttled the girl he had his orgasm. The connection while he was standing was merely a feigned manoeuvre. Butlies herself says: "I hardly felt anything. Kürten finished very quickly and showed me the way out of the wood." And Butlies was an expert in lechery.

Again, in the deposition of Wilbertz: "The intercourse on the bench scarcely succeeded, for I became frightened and thrust him away. He did me no harm. He accompanied me to Rath." Despite the small degree of violence used, Kürten claims to have achieved his purpose in this case, too. It was not always so easy, for sometimes the throttling was not sufficient to induce orgasm, then it was that Kürten proceeded to the all-too-certain method of shedding blood. To that end he resorted to stabbing with dagger or scissors, or to hammer blows on the head of his victim. Later on, I shall refer again to this *modus operandi* in more detail when I come to the medico-legal consideration of the wounds.

In the account of the crime which Kürten gave to the police, he uses the following words: "It came to *sexual intercourse*." Several witnesses confirm this. Kürten, in fact, used two methods to achieve sexual gratification. Either he abandoned from the start the idea of actual intercourse, and this was in the greater number of cases, the arsons and the simple throttlings, or he resorted to an attack on the genitals of the victim by gripping under her skirt or by rough handling of her vulva. As has been remarked, the coitus was often merely a sham maneuver of Kürten's, but in some cases he did achieve coitus by violence as he confessed and as was proved. For example, with Reuter and Albermann. The explanation here, we may believe, was desire for change: *variatio delectat*. Kürten was unable to suggest to me a convincing motive. Reuter and Hahn were, as he put it, women who were out for marriage. But the child Albermann? Even so, in those cases where Kürten began coitus he only succeeded in penetration, while ejaculation was possible for him only when accompanied by violence. With Reuter this was by successive blows on the head; with Albermann by countless stabs in the breast.

The *return* to the scenes of his crimes was also a plain sexual urge. Kürten rejects this idea for he does not desire it to be believed that it was his sexual lust that impelled him to it, and as a motive suggests his atonement idea. But when one makes him talk freely about it, then he reveals himself as to his sadistic excitation: "I went, over and over again, to the graves of the victims, returned repeatedly to Mülheim to the grave of Klein and to the StofFeler cemetery. When I fingered the earth of the grave with my hand I sometimes became sexually excited, and when I recalled in memory the events, I could stay for hours by the grave of Hahn. But when I had an orgasm on the graves it was without any act on my part. The great thing was that I was within reach of the achievement of my mission."

It appears to have been the rule that he tried to find new sexual stimulants by looking at the scenes of his crimes: "The place where I attacked Frau Kühn I visited again that same evening twice, and also later several times. In doing so I sometimes had an orgasm. When that morning I poured petrol over the child Ohliger and set fire to her, I had an orgasm at the height of the fire. The scene of that crime I visited again the same morning at half-past-eight and half-past-nine, and later on, frequently."

I do not want to close this chapter regarding Kürten's sadism without mentioning that Kürten occasionally gave himself up to a desire for pain. He says himself that he irritated and made angry some of the women in order to provoke them to strike him. There might also be a masochistic component in the

achievement of an orgasm by the defence of these victims. I
have in mind the Santo case where the throttled woman
kicked vigorously, and the attacked woman who broke her
umbrella over his head.

CHAPTER V
KÜRTEN'S CHARACTER PATTERN
AND SOME ASPECTS OF CRIMINAL PSYCHOLOGY

I will begin this chapter with the observation that, following twelve months of observation, Kürten was not in my view mad in the sense of Paragraph 51, St G.B. (Criminal Code). The psychiatral observations of him in the mental institution led me to the same conclusion. Neither can we regard Kürten's crimes as compulsive acts committed in a condition amounting to unconsciousness within the meaning of the Paragraph referred to above.

Our definition of the true compulsive act is such act as proceeds from a conscious motive, but passes from its mental phase to the deed itself without any weighing of the pros and cons. Even were one to assume that the urge in Kürten was abnormally strong, he yet, assuredly, comes short of irresistible compulsion. One must certainly agree that Kürten felt in himself the sexual urge most powerfully, more strongly than another man easily excited. In 1929 already he noted the extraordinary increase of the urge. Once he said to me: "I wonder what it was, that urge to go out, that demon which drew me out every evening without exception? It is no merit of mine that it did not happen a lot more. When I wasn't able to go out because my wife was at home, I sometimes raged with impatience. I *had* to go out, and to get out even if it came only to visiting the woods where I paced up and down in lonely parts, conjuring up in my mind my old crimes." Fundamentally, it was no more than a habit, this going out in the evening and on holidays to seek for a suitable victim. If he did not find one, and that was, fortunately, the rule, then he only went home unsatisfied. If there was any hindrance, or any danger of discovery interfered with the execution of his sadistic purpose, then he backed down very quickly from its execution. That much he has admitted himself of the several interrupted attacks. Even at his sexual climax he was extremely alert and ready to run for instant safety. The Schulte case (59) illustrates that point well. Kürten had stabbed this girl in rapid succession, the orgasm was achieved, when the whole neighbourhood woke up and Kürten ran away. The attack on Radusch furnishes another example (62). Kürten ran away so quickly that he ejaculated into his clothing.

The sadism of Kürten is a perversion of the sex impulse in an abnormal psychic constitution. Kürten is a psychopath: the unfortunate biological inheritance from drunken father and grandfather came out in him in all sorts of character deficiencies and in the abnormality of this urge. Thus born in him was the predisposition for the deviation of the sexual urge, the conditioning of the direction of that urge by early experiences, and the abnormal excitation of feeling which produces lust, and by impressions and fantasies which in another would have awakened only feelings of repugnance. The sadism of Kürten is thus a perversion budded from the total personality, which is psychically abnormal. His sadism is, in part, a symptom of a genuine psychopathy because it is the one single component in his degenerate being which swamps and dominates all the others.

I have already indicated the close link between sadism and *cruelty*, Kürten himself realized it in the course of his medical examinations by various physicians. Towards the end of these medical observations he told me of another memory of his childhood which I would like to mention.

At the age of nine he often played with other boys on the logs which were tied together as rafts and anchored near the banks of the Rhine near Mülheim.

They loved to ride on the floating logs. Once he pushed under his raft a boy who had happened to fall off his log into the shallow water so that he was drowned. Another time he threw a boy from the extreme edge of the raft into the Rhine. This boy, too, was carried away on the tide and drowned. In doing these things he was well aware that he was doing something wrong, but he had an agreeable feeling while doing them.

Though Kürten was subjected to a rigid discipline by his father, he became *criminal* very young — at the age of sixteen. Once cast into the ways of crime, he was unable to return. One larceny followed upon another, sentences became

longer and longer, until, at last, he was sent to the penitentiary
for long terms of penal servitude.

Only in 1921, in his thirty-eighth year, a change came over
him. He came under the influence of a woman of great will-
power. He began to live a hardworking life. The burglaries
stopped. But the sadistic urges remained undiminished and
showed themselves in an ever increasing way until the Year of
the Terror, in 1929.

The other psychopathic tendencies of Kürten kept themselves
within reasonable bounds. His inclination to *lie* and *deceive* he
cultivated to unheard-of mastery. Otherwise he could not
possibly have hidden his crimes from his wife and all the
world for so long a time. This histrionic art of dissimulation
was such that his mask of a respectable citizen and of a gallant
cavalier was scarcely penetrable.

It gave him the assurance which enabled him to lure his
victims away and to keep them quiet until the moment of
attack. This bearing of his is backed by a stupendous presence
of mind and bluff. In the most complicated of situations he
finds his way out. His wife surprises him with a strange girl:
by a joking word he saves the situation for himself. Again: the
girl Schäfer, scared by the repeated attempts to throttle her
(Case 6), asks the waitress of the beer garden for protection.
Kürten disarms suspicion at once with the words: "She is my
bride. If she has her moods, you need not take them
seriously."

The girl from Heme, having luckily escaped from being
throttled, later recognizes him in the street and would have
him arrested. Kürten rids himself of her with a very assured
gesture. This assurance in his bearing Kürten acquired through
the long years of a criminal career. After all, he had been for
years a professional burglar, and he had made a specialty, as
an expert housebreaker, of entering houses where the
householder would be known to be downstairs attending to his
business, that of inn-keeper. The cases of Klein and Franken
show how cold-bloodedly he worked.

In bizarre contrast to his mendacity there appears sometimes a
brutal frankness; it is a sadistic feature, as though he desired

to savour the terror of his victim. "Now there will be a horrible end," he said to Schäfer. And to Hau, after having kissed the blood from her lips: "You can congratulate yourself that we are not alone in the Hofgarten." The queer mixture of mendacity and frankness in Kürten's make-up does certainly force the observer to approach his confessions with great caution. It was this that drew out the preliminary investigations and caused them to last for more than six months.

The Public Prosecutor noticed that Kürten lied often out of his sadistic impulses, in order to get witnesses into trouble. If possible, he wished to involve them in proceedings for perjury. On the other hand, whoever wins Kürten's confidence, as we physicians did during the investigation, must be astonished at the complete accessibility of this strange man. I am convinced that as far as I am concerned Kürten held nothing back. On the contrary, he had an active desire to reveal himself to me. Of this I will give an example. He spoke of his reactions to the many physicians who had him under observation and finished with the words: "When Professor X was here for the first time, he brought his lady assistant with him, and she had such a lovely white neck that I would have loved to have strangled it. Once, when the Professor left the room, leaving me alone with her, I had to keep myself in hand. This sort of thing came over me suddenly often enough, as, for instance, at Mülheim."

Another outstanding characteristic of Kürten's was his vanity. He set great store by his personal appearance. His fellow-workmen noticed how he cleaned himself up thoroughly, and even made-up before a mirror. When he went for a walk he carried a duster for his shoes. When I had to examine Kürten's clothing for blood stains the room in my laboratory looked like a tailor's shop, so lavishly was Kürten provided with suits. And every suit was well kept, each pair of trousers carefully creased. Every spot had been removed, so that I could detect blood only in the seams of those trouser pockets in which he had carried his murderous instruments. His smartness, his well-cared-for person, was noticed by all the girls and as he had a slim figure, fresh-complexioned face and plentiful hair, all thought him much younger than his age. The witnesses thought him twenty-five to twenty-eight or thirty. This exterior appearance was the mirror of the man himself, a complacency that can be gauged both by speech and deeds. This complacency played a decisive part in his confession. Already at the time of the arrest of Stausberg he claimed to have been engaged in conjuring up the scene when the moment would come when he would reveal himself to the much-lauded criminal police: *I am the criminal!* He himself says quite openly that he was urged by *megalomania* to give the list of his crimes. From the amazed and troubled faces of his auditors he read their growing horror and astonishment as the list proceeded, apparently without end. Even in his braggadoccio a perverse sense of humour lay concealed. Finally, the manner in which he described his crimes and motivated them is in itself a demonstration of megalomania. Kürten's vengeance motive was not a free invention and must therefore be considered in addition to the sexual motive. Disciples of Freud will experience no surprise on hearing that Kürten mentioned frequently his wounded feelings and sense of injustice from the start of his examination. In the opinion of the psychoanalysts the criminal differs from the man who adjusts himself to society and the rule of law in a normal way, in that he fails to sublimate the aggressive primitive urges; or, to use the terminology of Freud himself, that the super ego (that is, the moral conscience) is lacking as a decisive factor to influence the ego. The primitive urges remain in the criminal with undiminished vigor and from this develops the disharmony, the tension, between the instinctual life and the moral social existence. Tensions like this, which are abreacted by the common neurotic by nervous symptoms of disease, force the criminal neurotic to crime. He then motivates his actions by the wounds inflicted upon him by injustice: Society, the Law, has treated me unjustly, therefore I am justified in acting against its norms. Kürten has assured me, over and over again, that he occupied himself with such thoughts in the solitude of the years of his imprisonments.

Along with his sadistic fantasies, they were a consolation to him for the long deprivations of his liberty. This feature he has in common with many criminals. One need only refer to those who have used this method in their memoirs, for example, the infamous Monalescu claimed that by his larcenies he had only executed the vengeance of the poor on the rich, that his life and actions had been a moral struggle with human society. Basically, the idea of vengeance and atonement in Kürten's case is rooted in sadism. With him it is merely a mask for the sexual feeling. After the various hearings by legal experts and physicians were completed, I asked him once whether he felt more appeased now.

He said: "Yes, I am sobered up. I also see that the idea of vengeance and atonement was wrong. For hours I sat beside the graves of my victims to give myself up to this idea. The sexual side of this remained in the background, yet it came into the picture. For instance, I had, as I have already told you, fingered the earth on the grave of Klein. I could imagine from the picture which was affixed to the grave what the child looked like, with her tresses that hung forward over her shoulders. Thinking of that I ejaculated. It was the same at the grave of Hahn. I went at least eight to twenty times within three months to the Brachfeld. Over and over again I was drawn to it. That sort of thing, of course, you understand as a criminologist — that the criminal always returns to the scene of his crime. Whenever I fingered the graves I always had an orgasm again. I was even drawn there when I went for a walk with my wife who, for her part, wished to go to Grafenberg, while, as for me, I was impelled to take the other direction to Papendell, in order to visit Halm's grave. Again, when I went for a walk with my father, I was drawn to the places where I had met Ohliger and Scheer. And when I visited those spots alone I had an orgasm on recalling the things that had happened there."

In this account the true character of Kürten's revenge motive reveals itself as ninety per cent sadism, ten per cent sense of injustice. Even so, since Kürten came back to it again and again throughout our discussions, I record it here. The effect

of *auto-suggestion* is, above all, a remarkable feature with Kürten. The solitude of the prison cell developed in him the power to achieve orgasm purely by indulgence in sadistic fantasies. We know from other cases the danger of suggestion by pornography or cinema performances and also by press reports of the full details of sexual crimes. Kürten, too, says himself that this sort of reading had an effect on him:
"I always got the papers, all of them, and as they were displayed it cost me nothing. In particular I read the murder stories. In doing so I always got sexually excited. Besides that, there were always people about the displayed newspapers in whose faces I saw horror." (In answer to my question) "Yes, sometimes I ejaculated. I have read Jack the Ripper several times and I also liked to go to the cinema where exciting pictures were displayed showing somebody being gripped by the neck or thrown over a cliff."
In addition to these means, Kürten always kept his sadistic instinctual life going by the stimulation of his *waking fantasies*. Even now he is able to relieve the tedium of imprisonment by this exuberant fantasy weaving.
On the 31st of October, 1930, Kürten asked that I should visit him. "I want to ask you another question, Professor," he said. "Do you think they are finished with their investigation? I wanted to tell you that I have often heard voices and often I thought I saw great throngs of people from my house and heard music. The Oberbürgmeister was making a speech and after him the Police President in honour of the police officer who had captured the Düsseldorf murderer. It was so real that I thought I actually heard the voices. With one ear I actually heard: with the other I dreamed. I was sometimes a man divided into two halves."
Besides these more or less pathological features Kürten had notable qualities of character and talent. The reader will recognize his uncommon mental processes in the statements given above verbatim. One sees how Kürten took advantage of every chance to enlarge his general education; and he has certainly come to amazing depths of knowledge of human nature and adjustment to environment. The foundation for this

is to be found in his good *memory*.

A comparative examination of his statements of dates with the records of the fire departments showed that not only did Kürten give the right date, but the exact minute. If one listens to him describing meticulously the interiors of some of the scenes of his crimes, for example, the Klein's, at Mülheim, which he entered seventeen years ago, and if one then compares his detailed description with the sketch made for the investigating magistrate, one can only marvel at the astounding quality of his memory.

Kürten had very sharp eyes for every minor circumstance. To mention but one: he gauged the monetary status of his victims after knowing them only a short time. In 1913 he broke into the home of the Frankens in the evening, saw the daughter lying in bed and throttled her. Seventeen years later he said that there were three beds in the room and estimated the age of the throttled girl at sixteen or seventeen years. Actually, Gertrud Franken was born in 1896 and was thus seventeen years old.

Kürten's swift appreciation of each perilous situation gives the real explanation of his long immunity from arrest. Heindl (The Professional Criminal, page 225) draws attention to another reason why murderers remain undetected so frequently. Murderers are usually skilled criminals, old soldiers in a warfare waged perpetually with the police. The professional murderer has usually been first for many years a burglar or criminal of some other kind. Occasionally, in the act of burglary, the criminal comes under the necessity of killing so that no witness should remain of his crime. From that point forward murder comes within the frame of the burglar's calculations from the inception of a fresh crime. He then kills deliberately and as a professional killer.

As, according to Heindl, even the mediocre murderer is superior to the police, how much more must that be the case with an expert assassin like Kürten? I do not want to omit reference to the fact that during his long imprisonment awaiting trial, Kürten got a different angle on his crimes from that which he had had at the beginning. At the end he showed,

if not regret, at least a more serious view. He said to me in
January, 1931:

"The preliminary investigation is now over; the trial will
probably open in April. I am in favour of a quiet sort of trial. I
will ask that the public be excluded, so that youths shall not
read the reports in the papers. I know from my own case how
such reports of sexual crimes aggravated me. I have heard,
too, in the streets how even quite young girls are keen after
newspaper reports like these and how they promise chocolate
to each other if one of them can secure the latest report in the
final editions. Yes, at the Wehrhahn I once heard a pupil — I
think from the girls' college — saying: 'I would rather like to
go with him once, if I was only sure he wouldn't harm me.'
She referred to the Düsseldorf murderer. I need only think of
the trials of Krantz, Guttmann, Husmann, and of the damage
done by the newspaper reports, to want to have the public
excluded for the sake of my family and my wife."

Kürten never showed actual remorse: "How could I do so?
After all, I had to fulfil my mission," he said.

On another occasion he said: "If I was let loose today I
couldn't guarantee that I would not immediately do something
again. I can't feel remorse, but only regret for the innocent
victims. Up to to-day, I have felt no remorse. I could not act
differently."

To the prison chaplain Kürten said in his last days that he
could not understand how he had been able to kill the child
Albermann. The child had been so sweet to him, and when he
carried her, she put her little arms about his neck. In short, she
was so trustful. Kürten thought a lot about himself and got to
the point of some sort of self-recognition. He calls himself
impetuous to the point of brutality; speaks often of his
inclination to brag, of the megalomania which is inherited in
his family. He is aware of his fatal sadistic propensity. All
this, he explains, is due to heredity and his horrible youth.

"What a man becomes has nothing to do with him. It's just
what his parents were; and that applies to me, too. Just for the
pleasure of being bad no man becomes a criminal, there is
always a certain something which comes into it and for which

he is not answerable." It is also of interest that in the last months before his trial, Kürten occupied himself in prison with the question of his *legal responsibility*.

In February, 1931, he said to me: "I must come back to the question about which we have talked already. Paragraph 51 (of the Criminal Code) does not come into question with me. The reports from you, from Bedburg and of Professor Sioli say as much. I have already explained to you, Professor, how I felt before, during and after the execution of my crimes — well, do you think it impossible that there was a pathological predisposition? The urge was so strong that I could not resist it. And there is another thing that has to do with Paragraph 51, something rather out of the ordinary. Though I take it as it comes now — I mean with regard to the execution and so on — the question whether I really had free will remains open." (Note in these words, taken down verbatim, the clever way of expressing himself that Kürten had acquired during those later months by frequent exchanges with legal experts and physicians.) In this way Kürten wished to suggest that he was impelled to the commission of his sexual crimes, for, quite rightly, he recognized that it was from there that the whole question of legal responsibility derived.

Magnus Hirschfeld has pleaded in speech and writing for a far-reaching exculpation of sexual criminals of the type of Kürten, and has stated his fundamental propositions in his *Sexual Pathology* (2nd Edition).

"All the lust murderers," he wrote, "who have been examined up to the present time by competent experts were psychopaths of a marked degenerate type. Only in a single case was there any question whether the hereditary bias is sufficiently strong to restrain the pathological impulses. In most cases this is to be denied."

Ought one to accept Kürten's statements without critical examination? If so, then one should deny this in his case also, and question his responsibility. But I am of the opinion that the problem cannot be boiled down to so simple a formula as Hirschfeld does. And I think, too, the psycho-pathology and, indeed, the entire spiritual personality, and not only the instinctual life, must be taken into account.

Kürten's sadistic urges did not permit pity to stand between him and his victims. Only once there seems to be a glimmer of it — when he said to Bell, when she invited him to repeat the sexual act with her, that she was wasted on him as he was a bad man. One might think that Kürten, when for the last time he was together with his wife (Friday, 23.5.1930), broke down under the burden of remorse and that he craved freedom from this burden by a confession in some sort of mood of repentance. His wife shared this belief.

Kürten again and again denied this collapse, described so convincingly by his wife. But his reason for the denial was clear: it was to render convincing his idea of atonement, his mission. A psychic collapse does not fit well into this scheme for the presentation of a cool composed hero who remains constant to the voluntary termination of his mission. Generally speaking, Kürten is inclined to hide behind ironic remarks certain emotions.

Another one attempting to build up from the published reports of his crimes the manner of man Kürten must have been, imagines him as a cold, crude man, a very beast in human shape. But the reader of a newspaper only hears or reads of the horrible. It is otherwise with one who was occupied more closely with this extraordinary man. Thus one is able to distinguish between the sadist Kürten and the man Kürten, and make the discovery that, aside from his defects, Kürten possessed qualities similar in every way to the ordinary run of men. A kind and accessible chatterer, with a wide general knowledge and with sound judgement, he made one forget that the man who faced us was the Düsseldorf murderer ... In this there is, after all, nothing very remarkable, for according to Magnus Hirschfeld, the majority of sadists have been weaklings and pampered persons, and often, indeed, even of such kindly disposition that nobody would have believed them capable of such crimes.

CHAPTER VI
THE MEDICO-LEGAL LESSONS OF THE KÜRTEN CASE

(A) THE WOUNDS OF THE VICTIMS.

From the medico-legal standpoint I know of no more interesting personality in criminology than Kürten. The explanation, as I see it, is his many sidedness. I have already referred to the fact that sadistic criminals, just as with professional criminals, usually adhere to identical methods of crime. Kürten indulged in every form of sadistic perversion known to us; from indulgence in fantasies of sadism and the simulated throttling which was used as an ancillary means of excitation in normal coitus, to the substitution actions of simple stabbing, blood seeing, arson, to the actual lust murder. He even varies the lust murder in two peculiar ways, either by stabbing to kill, while actually copulating, or by attempting to obtain orgasm by brutalities without attempting coitus. In no case did he first murder his victim, and thereafter indulge in coitus with the dead. Necrophilia is foreign to him. His dealings with Hahn must not be regarded in this light, either. Though he ejaculated when he dragged her body into the ditch, the excitement was actually stimulated by the carrying of the body and the thoughts which engaged his imagination that he would nail it to a tree.

Thus we see that Kürten carried out the lust murder as a killing during the sexual act in the cases of Reuter, Dörrier, and Albermann, and as killing as substitute for the sexual act in the cases of Scheer, Hamacher, and Lenzen. In between these two, come the lust murders of a transitory character — killings with violation of the vagina in the cases of Klein and Ohliger. Violations of the vagina were of a serious kind only in the case of Klein, the child being torn open from the perineum to the rectum.

Kürten, describing what he did, says that he drilled his right hand into the vagina with the extended fingers together. In the case of the child Ohliger, only a small laceration in the mucous membrane of the vestibulum was found, caused, obviously, by the nail when Kürten tried to dig his finger into the vagina. Kürten cannot explain the violation of the vagina of Dörrier, which bears a marked resemblance to the injury of Ohliger, save that it is bigger and deeper. In the case of the Albermann child, it is explained by the introduction of the penis. The explanation of the absence of copious bleeding from these wounds is to be found in the diminished force of the hearts of these dying victims.

Of greater importance are those wounds which proved fatal or nearly fatal. In four cases Kürten used the throat-cutting method; twice with fatal results (Klein and Hamacher) and twice without (Lenzen and Schulte). In each case the wounds were inflicted only after several attempts. In the case of Schulte, the throat wounds were unsuccessful because suffocation, which usually supervenes, was absent, for the girl was a grown adult. The throat wounds in the case of the fourteen-year-old Lenzen were superficial, probably because the girl recovered consciousness after being throttled and began to defend herself.

Kürten was unable to give a coherent account of this, as he was in some other cases. He has, at the climax, an unreliable memory. For instance, he remembers nothing of the throat-cutting of Lenzen, but only the stabbing in the back. To cut the throat of Klein he used a small penknife, the blade of which was not more than 4 cm. in length, but was kept so sharp that Kürten could cut the end of his cigar with the slightest pressure.

(B) THE STAB WOUNDS.

I have repeatedly expressed my conviction that for Kürten the killing was not an end in itself, but the method whereby he secured the bleeding which was his main purpose. The blow, the stab, these were far more important for him than any consequences that flowed from them. That is why he stabbed and stabbed or struck and struck again. By considering the significance of the numerous stabs or blows upon the bodies of the victims, we can estimate, in each case, how long it took Kürten to achieve his end — an orgasm. (He said: "At the beginning of the ill treatment there was never any ejaculation, that is why I had to go on stabbing.") Hence the innumerable stabs on the body of Albermann (Case 67), where a button of the coat of the child showed more than a dozen stab marks. Here the number is accounted for by the position of Kürten when he inflicted the wounds. According to his own account, he was in the act of coitus when he realized the slackening of his erection. He therefore commenced to stab in order to stimulate his organ. On the other hand, in the case of the child Lenzen (Case 58), four stabs sufficed to secure ejaculation, and that although but a few moments had passed since the ejaculation which followed his murder of the child Hamacher. In the case of Kornblum, ejaculation apparently followed on the first stab; but this stab followed on the stabbing of Goldhausen and Mantel, and thus added to an accumulation of sadistic irritation. In the method of his stabbing Kürten differs entirely from other known sadistic stabbers who turn up periodically in various parts. The so-called Berlin Stabber directed his stabs to the abdomens of the girls; the Hip-stabber of Metz wounded twenty-three girls, all within a brief period, all in the same neighbourhood and always with the same needle-like tool. It was soon after these atrocities that a similar hip-stabber appeared in Trier. The most notorious case on record is that of the stabber of Augsburg, whose arrest took place only after eighteen years, during which period he had stabbed fifty girls. (Wulffen, in his *Handbook of Sexual Delinquency*), provides much case literature under this head.) Kürten gave us many problems to solve in the interpretation of the wounds of his victims by changing the stabbing tools. In the attacks on Kühn, Ohliger, Hahn, and Albermann, he used the scissors, stabbing with a wide-open scissor, like a dagger which he drove into his victim. In addition to superficial stabs that merely punctured the skin, there were stabs that penetrated both heart and lungs. The point of the scissors was broken in the skull of Frau Kühn and healed in, undetected. It was only through Kürten's confession that our

117

attention was drawn to it. An X-ray photograph showed the point of the scissors embedded in the skull on the crown of the head. In the three other cases enumerated, Kürten took a second pair of scissors, the blades of which were 85 mm. long and, at their broadest point, 12.5 mm. wide. He used scissors because his cautious criminal nature appreciated the fact that while a dagger, found in his flat, would have been deadly evidence against him, a simple pair of household scissors, carefully cleaned after each outrage, could cause no suspicion at all.

Kürten, at one time, however, did use a dagger, wounding by that method Goldhausen, Mantel, Kornblum, the Flehe children, and Schulte. The numerous wounds confirm established medico-legal experience: namely, that no certain conclusion can be drawn from the length and width of wounds. It is a different affair with the stabs of the children Ohliger and Albermann. A comparison of the pictures reveals the coincidence in direction, position, and size of the stabs. The almost complete absence of movement of the moribund victims and the rapid stabs with the scissors, account for the fact that the withdrawal of the blade did not widen the place of entry. From the number of the stabs and their uniformity of size (12 mm.) one could estimate the width of the blade. On the other hand, no reliable conclusion as to the length of the blade is to be arrived at by the measurement of the stab channel. The maximum length of the blade which inflicted the injuries was no more than 8.5 cm. The difference, an apparent disparity, is explained by the compression of the tissues of the flesh of the breast.

During the post mortem examinations we expected to find — assuming the weapon to have been an ordinary knife — contusion about the edges of the wounds, since great force had so obviously been used. This expectation was based on the fact that the haft of the knife would inevitably inflict such external injury. By a series of experiments upon bodies we came to the conclusion that for the complete absence of contusion, we must assume a knife of a very special kind, a knife, somewhat similar to the scalpel, whose haft tapers and thus offers no obstacle whereby the skin is bruised in .the act of stabbing. A scissor stab produces two effects: it tends to lessen bruising about the lips of the wounds, secondly it produces a false idea of the wounds' depth, the tissues of the breast yielding before the pressure of the blade.

The specific form of the wounds in the skulls of Hamacher and Albermann is determined by the scissors blade. Stabbing experiments with Kürten's scissors into the skull bones of children and persons of the same age, yielded holes of the same shape. The reason why they were not recognized as scissor wounds at the autopsies is that we had already in our possession knives with backs ground off on one side, and such a knife, we assumed, had been used in the case of Hahn and Albermann. We had experience of wounds caused by scissors used in the closed position; but it was something new to us that a criminal might use a scissors with the blades separated, and, therefore, such a possibility did not enter into our calculations. Later, by a series of experiments, I convinced myself that stabs from ordinary household scissors, one blade being used, leave not always, but generally, peculiar slits in the skin of the body, slits with a pointed end which corresponds to the edge of the blade. The other end, also pointed, has a slight twist that gives it the appearance of a beak. (Plate 5.) The illustration represents several wounds of entry which I have copied from the Albermann child's front breast wall, which is preserved at the Institute. These drawings are slightly enlarged. It will be seen that in each case here illustrated, the left edge of each wound conforms to the shape of the scissors-blade back.

From the foregoing considerations, it follows that a scissors blade can leave behind characteristic wounds of entry in the skin surface. But not all scissor blades give such peculiar, beaklike punctures.

(C) OF THE THROTTLING.

The most illuminating of all the sadistic proclivities of Kürten from the medico-legal point of view is the throttling. He used

the throttling grip in a dual way. Either he gripped his victim suddenly by the throat in the middle of a conversation and throttled her, or he persuaded her to the sexual act and throttled her while performing it. According to his own statement and the evidence of the surviving victims, he throttled violently and persistently. His major purpose in doing this was to stimulate himself sexually to orgasm; but also to prevent the woman from shouting or running away. For these reasons the throttling grip had to be applied very firmly. Maria Maas, who was able to free herself very quickly from his throttling grip and run away, said: "For days one could see on my throat the five marks of his nails."
He, himself, described his procedure thus: "I always did this throttling in the same way. I always got to the right-hand side of the girl, then suddenly seized her neck with the right hand in front and the left behind, hooked my crooked fingers round the gullet and pressed hard. If the first grip is placed properly one can say that one has succeeded; that means that the victims were not able to shout. I always gripped for five minutes. That did not happen in two minutes! Even with a child it takes about two minutes, for instance, with Ohliger. If the grip is not applied properly, then the opportunity is lost, for the girls screamed. The girl from Heme screamed so loudly behind Belzen Platz that the whole neighbourhood reechoed. I never knew a case where the victim became unconscious right away. So, too, with the children in Flehe, they struggled and defended themselves with their arms. Ohliger also beat about with her arms. Even when she was on the ground and already unconscious, she still struggled with her legs."

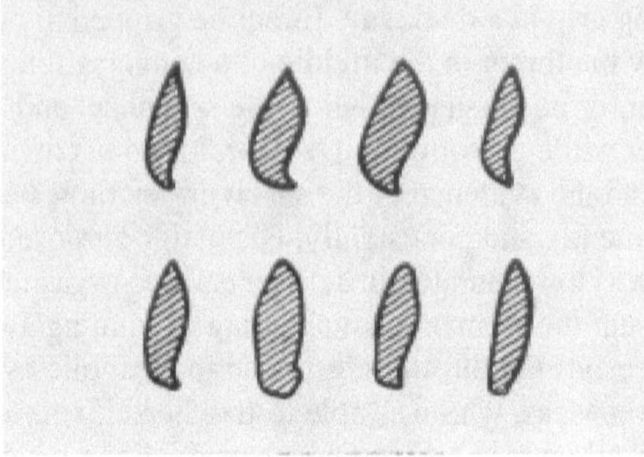

PLATE 5
SCISSOR BREAST WOUNDS
(Albermann case)

(Those were, of course, the cramps of suffocation.)
When I asked Kürten whether death had followed on the
throttling alone, he said that he believed that the children
Ohliger, Hamacher, Albermann, and Klein would have died,
even without the wounds inflicted afterwards. Furthermore, he
is of the opinion that he throttled Anni to death and threw her
into the Rhine when she was already dead. This case could not
be cleared up. No female body corresponding to Kürten's
description was recovered from the Rhine in the Düsseldorf
Valley; neither did the Dutch river officials have anything to
report about it. Last, nowhere was an "Anni" reported
missing. Throughout the whole of the hearings Kürten
adhered with such positiveness to his statements that I do not
accept these objections as evidence that Kürten was lying. The
Rhine usually gives up her summer bodies. Yet I have had
myself, in my Institute, the body of a woman who had been
embedded for a whole year in the mud of the river bank and
who came to light only because of an extraordinary drought.
Kürten described to me in a quite detached way, the
proceedings at the killing of Anni.
"I could describe the girl in detail. She had brown hair and
such fat breasts. I throttled her for at least five minutes with
both hands. I let go of her throat because she struggled for
121

such a long time. It was while I was doing this that I had an
orgasm. I thought she was dead as she hung down so limply."
Kürten knew well the signs of death. A few days earlier he
had handled the body of Hahn and a five minutes' throttling
may well lead to death. Again, the description of the deed
itself need not be regarded as a fabrication, for all the other
crimes, save a few lying far back, which could not be either
proved or disproved — were proved by examination to have
been described minutely. I therefore think it probable that
Anni was throttled by him.

Kürten reported, also in detail, a failure: "I did not succeed in
throttling Hahn. I had throttled her firmly with both hands and
I knelt by her on the right side, thus pressing the whole weight
of my body on her throat for four minutes at least.
Nevertheless, she recovered consciousness. Then I throttled
her again, though not for so long as the first time. She did not
die even then. When I stabbed her throat the blood spurted
out. After I had stabbed her in the breast I heard the blood
gushing through her blouse. It was only then that I had the
orgasm."

In the list on the following page, the throttling cases are listed
according to the outcome of the throttling. Taking them as an
experimental group, we are able to draw some conclusions. To
deal first with their negative characteristics we note that there
are no deaths from shock in the list. All the victims struggled
for minutes against the murderer. I assume that during the
incessant throttling grip pressure on the carotids in their
different sections had been exerted. Although with some of
the throttled Hering's Coefficient of the onset of suffocation
was just becoming evident, no heart failure occurred. In none
of the twenty-four cases was a success quickly secured, not
even with the children. According to Kürten's own statement
the resistance was maintained for minutes long. (Kürten's
timing was always found to be reliable whenever we were
able to check it up.)

There was unconsciousness following the throttling in nine
cases out of the twenty-four. It must remain an open question
whether of these nine victims throttled to the point of

unconsciousness any would have died without the infliction of the stabs which followed. The first throttling case on the list, that of 1899, did not end fatally, despite unconsciousness and apparent death. The seven fatal cases showed besides suffocation vital reactions to their death wounds; therefore, it is clear that they were not killed directly by the throttling. It must remain a question whether Anni went into the Rhine as a corpse. Thus, the somewhat singular fact emerges that of the twenty four throttled persons none has been certainly killed by this means:

TABLE II

	Name	Case	Outcome of Throttling	Details
1	Klein	7	Unconsciousness	Fatal throat cut
2	Ohliger	46	Unconsciousness	Fatal stabbing
3	Hamacher	57	Unconsciousness	Fatal throat cut
4	Lenzen	58	Unconsciousness	Fatal stabbing
5	Albermann	67	Unconsciousness	Fatal stabbing
6	Hahn	52	Unconsciousness	Fatal stabbing
7	Anni	53	Unconsciousness	Fatal throttling
8	Unknown	1	Unconsciousness	Left for dead
9	Franken	11	Unconsciousness	Criminal surprised
10	Schäfer	7	Without Result	Throttling during coitus
11	Tiede	14	Without Result	Throttling during coitus
12	Mech	15	Without Result	Throttling during coitus
13	Ist	22	Without Result	Throttling during coitus
14	Hilde	68	Without Result	Throttling during coitus
15	Wil	71	Without Result	Throttling during coitus
16	Wack	17	Without Result	Struggled free
17	Kiefer	16	Without Result	Struggled free
18	Maas	50	Without Result	Struggled free
19	Freitag	51	Without Result	Struggled free
20	Rad	62	Without Result	Struggled free
21	Santo	69	Without Result	Struggled free
22	Becker	70	Without Result	Struggled free
23	Heme	72	Without Result	Struggled free
24	Hau	73	Without Result	Struggled free

Let us look at these twenty-four cases regarded as an experimental group in order to examine the applicability of

Hering's Theory of the stimulation of the carotid sinus. It is known that Hering in his experiments with animals produced extra systoles by compressing the bulb of the carotids and that he also produced ventricular fibrillation when other factors were present in addition to stimulation of the sinus.
Hering also regards commencing suffocation as one of these factors. Lochte has pleaded the applicability of Hering's theory to forensic medicine. Haberda cites Hering's view without supporting it with a single case out of his rich experience. It is certain that there are among Kürten's cases those in which Hering's conditions for death from heart failure were fulfilled, yet not a single instance of death from heart failure is given among them. Kürten, who was an extremely good observer, had described in the fatal cases the typical symptoms of suffocation up to the convulsions of suffocation. Recently, Hering (*Deutsche Medizinische Wochenschrift*, 1931, p. 530) drew attention to the fact that one must distinguish in a pressure experiment on the throat between the carotid sinus pressure experiment and the carotid pressure experiment.
The stimulation point for the latter lies deeper down on the carotid trunk. Both pressure experiments have a precisely contrary effect if carefully carried out, because sinus pressure augments and carotid pressure diminishes the parasympathetic tonus. This opposite effect of pressure applied at two points on the carotid fairly near together gives us the explanation of the absence of heart failure in the normal throttling grip. The four closed fingers have the effect of a sinus pressure and a carotid pressure at the same time, and therefore, exclude any effect on the reflex nervous control of the circulation.
The findings of the autopsies on the throttled victims of this list were so significant that they permitted the diagnosis of suffocation by violence. I have noted the anatomical symptoms of suffocation in the following table. It shows that although the same method of throttling may be used consistently, the anatomical result of it may be different.
The congestion of blood in the head was not present in the bodies of Hamacher and Lenzen, but it was quite distinct with

the three other children. In only one case was the protrusion of the tongue lacking. It is easily understood that owing to the elasticity of the youthful tissues, graver damage to the internal organs of the throat and the laceration of the intima of the carotids were lacking in all the children. The marks of throttling showed distinct impressions of nails only in the case of the child Klein.

In the other four cases only the ends of the fingers had left marks behind. This difference is accounted for by the length of the criminal's finger nails and by the fact that the position of the sleeping child Klein was extremely favourable for the throttling grip of the left hand.

TABLE III

Case	Livid marks	Post mortem staining	Protrusion of Tongue	Signs of strangulations	Bloodstains
Klein	+	+	+	+	+
Ohliger	+	+	-	+	-
Hamacher	-	-	+	+	+
Lenzen	-	-	+	+	-
Albermann	+	-	+	+	-

(D) OF THE HAMMER BLOWS.

Kürten gave it as a reason for the change of murder weapon his desire to keep up the appearance of a plurality of criminals. This intention he did actually achieve in so far that up to the time of his confession the theory that there were other criminals involved was seriously considered — at least until the bodies of Albermann and Hahn were found. His substitution of a hammer for the dagger was due to no other cause than that the dagger broke in the vertebrae of Schulte. For the following attacks he carried a hammer: Reuter, Dörrier, Meurer, and Wanders were struck with a hammer until this weapon split on the skull of the last-named. The hammer was very old and dilapidated. The weight of the iron head was 500 gr. The face was 27 by 27 mm. and octagonal with bevelled edges. The sides of the octagonal were of a

125

different height, 8 mm. on the bevelled edges, the larger edges being, respectively, 12, 15, 15, 17 mm.

Kürten stated in his confession that the hammer in the Wanders case flew out of his hand in the Hofgarten. A search was made where he indicated and the head of the hammer was found under last year's leaves. I was unable to trace any blood as it had lain so long under the damp leaves. I only succeeded in discerning traces of blood on the hinge of Kürten's scissors. The skin wounds which the hammer caused on the heads of the women were the well-known bursting wounds. Plate 3 shows the characteristic appearance of the head wounds of Reuter and Dörrier. In addition, in certain places the four-sided figure was present, plainly caused by the face of the hammer.

The star shape of the bursting wounds in the scalp which is mentioned in the text books as the usual shape of hammer blows I have not observed in any of these wounds: they were all simple fissure wounds, thirteen in the case of Reuter, eight in that of Dörrier, and three in the case of Meurer. Where the Plates show a starred wound, it is the result of repeated blows. Here and there I saw the right-angled impression of the hammer face in the case of Ulrich, but this was produced by another hammer.

In Plate 6 the hammer blows which can be seen on the scalp are projected on the hole fractures in the skulls of Reuter and Dörrier. The white octagonals which are reduced in the same scale as the skull sections are the photographic representation of the hammer face. They coincide with the actual breaches in the skull and are appropriately positioned. One can see on the single fracture lines of the skull the exact plastic impression of the hammer edges. Thus on both right sections of the skull the obtuse angles of the octagonals of the hammer outline lie parallel to the edges of the fractures.

These Plates show very clearly the number of the blows which Kürten delivered upon the heads of these two victims. He told me that he always struck first at the temple. This is the spot regarded generally as the most vulnerable. Obviously, Kürten delivered these blows with the utmost savagery. Almost every hole is a complete fracture. The effect of these blows is of interest: each of the four women was felled instantaneously by the first blow, but all of them speedily regained consciousness. Reuter and Dörrier regained consciousness when Kürten attempted coitus: both begged for their lives. In the case of Meurer Kürten contented himself with four blows, as he was fearful of being surprised, being generally apprehensive of the Hellweg which was fairly well frequented in the early hours of the evening. This explains the less grievous character of the fractures in this case. In the case of Wanders, after delivery of four blows, the head of the hammer flew off, leaving the splintered shaft in his hand. The minor damage to the brain itself in the cases of Dörrier and Reuter is surprising when the complete shattering of the temple bones is considered. When we bear in mind the dimensions of the face of the hammer, namely 27 to 28 mm., the frequency of the hole fracture is remarkable.

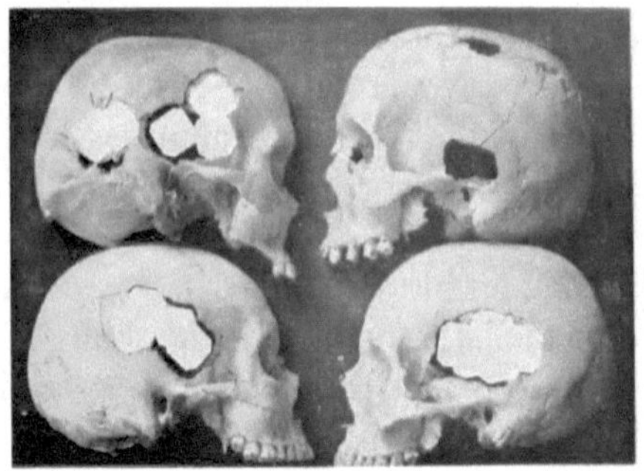

PLATE 6
SKULL HAMMER FRACTURES
(Reuter and Dörrier cases)

In 1888, Paltauf gave it as his opinion that only in cases where the hammer face did not exceed 14 by 16 mm. was a hole fracture likely to result. This view is not borne out by our cases. We have to remember that most hammers, irrespective of the size of the face, are convex; and we also have to bear in mind the fact that the surface of the skull at the point of

127

contact engages but a small part of the total hammer area.
Thus the underlying fallacy of the old theory is clearly seen.
This fact explains the small round hole fractures on the skull
of Reuter where only one segment of the convex hammer face
came into effective contact with one segment of the skull.
Of all the hammer cases, the most noteworthy was Case 77 so
far as the effects are concerned. Ulrich got the first hammer
blow on the left temple, the second against the right. Before
she became unconscious she put her hand instinctively to her
head and in that way protected it and lessened the effect of the
subsequent hammer blows. Kürten explained to me that he
had had an orgasm after several blows on seeing the gushing
blood and therefore desisted from further outrage.
Kürten's hammer was about the same size as the one he used
before and which broke in the Hofgarten. Although Ulrich had
sustained a depression fracture on either side of the skull she
remained unconscious for a short time only and then got up
unaided to seek help.

FINAL REMARKS.

After a hearing lasting ten days the jury of the Düsseldorf
Criminal Court found Kürten guilty of murder in nine cases.
In addition, he was found guilty of attempted murder in seven
cases. Despite Kürten's full confession, every crime was
investigated by the calling of witnesses during the trial.
Nothing beyond what I have set forth in the foregoing
chapters was revealed during the trial. Kürten behaved quietly
and in a dignified way. He did not challenge the death
sentence, did not feign remorse — which, in any case, he was
quite incapable of feeling — nor did he try to mitigate
anything. But he noted every discrepancy in the accounts of
the witnesses, and he also protested against the observations
of the Public Prosecutor and of the experts when they were
not, in his opinion, accurate. Most characteristic of all was his
final address at the close of the trial.

"As I now see the crimes committed by me, they are so ghastly that I do not want to attempt any sort of excuse for them. Still, I feel some bitterness when I think of the physician and the lady physician in Stuttgart who have been encouraged by a section of the community to murder and who have stained their hands with human blood to the extent of fifteen hundred murders. I do not want to accuse, all I want to do is to let you see what passes in my soul. I cannot refrain from reproaching you, Professor Sioli, for saying that the conditions of my home were not the decisive factor. On the contrary, you may well assume that youthful surroundings are decisive for the development of character. With silent longing I have sometimes in my early days glimpsed other families and asked myself why it could not be like that with us."

"I contradict the Chief Public Prosecutor when he asserts that it was out of cowardice that I revoked my confession. The very day that I opened up to my wife I well knew the consequences of the confession; I felt liberated in a certain way and I had the firm intention of sticking to my confession so that I could do a last good turn to my wife. But the real reason was that there arrives for every criminal that moment beyond which he cannot go. And I was in due course subject to this psychic collapse. As I have related already, I followed the reports in the newspapers then and, of course, later, very thoroughly. I convinced myself that on the whole the newspaper reports had been moderate. I may say that I used to intoxicate myself with the sensational press, it was the poison which must bear part of the responsibility of my poisoned life. By being moderate now, it has done a great deal to prevent the public from being poisoned. I feel urged to make one more statement: some victims made it rather easy for me to overpower them."

"I do not want to forget to mention what I frequently said before — that I detest the crimes and feel deep sorrow for the relatives. I even dare to ask those relatives to forgive me, as far as that may be possible for them. Furthermore, I want to point out emphatically that, contrary to the version of the Chief Public Prosecutor, I never tortured a victim. I do not attempt to excuse my crimes. I have already pointed out that I am prepared to bear the consequences of my misdeeds. I hope that thus I will atone for a large part of what I have done."

"Although I can suffer capital punishment only once, you may rest assured that it is one of the many unknown tortures to endure the time before the execution of the sentence, and dozens of times I have lived through the moment of the execution. And when you consider this and recognize my goodwill to atone for all my crimes. I should think that the terrible desire for revenge and hatred against me cannot endure. And I want to ask you to forgive me."

Kürten did not exercise his right of appeal, but he did put in a petition for pardon and thought that it would be successful, since the Minister of Justice then in office was an opponent of capital punishment. Towards the end of June I still found him full of hope for the pardon. Up to the last he always remained in his habitual mood, as is shown by the photograph which I took on the 18th of June in his cell. He expressed his joy in letters from his wife, and over the fact that four thousand marks of the reward offered for him had been paid to her. During the last month he made some response to the ministrations of the Church and he assured me that the waking fantasies, and the sadistic imagery of former times, had entirely vanished. He claimed that he was transformed into an entirely new being, although people outside might well not believe it.

On the 1st of July he received composedly news of the failure of his petition for pardon. Asked for his last wish, he asked to see his Düsseldorf confessor and for permission to write farewell letters. In the thirteen letters which he wrote to the relatives of his victims, he asked pardon and for their prayers, as he himself would pray for them in heaven.

Quietly and composedly, he went to the block on the 2nd of July, 1931.

PLATE 7
PETER KÜRTEN THREE DAYS BEFORE HIS EXECUTION

www.ingramcontent.com/pod-product-compliance
Lightning Source LLC
LaVergne TN
LVHW091510170726
843492LV00001B/424